Sweet Success

Additional copies may be ordered from the publisher for educational,
business, promotional or premium use.
For information, contact ALIVE Book Publishing at:
alivebookpublishing.com

Book design by Alex P. Johnson

ISBN 13
978-1-63132-239-6 Paperback
978-1-63132-240-2 Deluxe Color Harcover

Library of Congress Control Number: 2024917206

Library of Congress Cataloging-in-Publication Data
is available upon request.

First Edition

Published in the United States of America by ALIVE Book Publishing
an imprint of Advanced Publishing LLC
3200 A Danville Blvd., Suite 204, Alamo, California 94507
alivebookpublishing.com

PRINTED IN THE UNITED STATES OF AMERICA

10 9 8 7 6 5 4 3 2 1

Sweet
Success

How Industry, Immigrants, and
Working Women Shaped a Town

Barbara Pagni Denton

ABOOKS

Alive Book Publishing

LITTLE TOWN

I LIKE TO LIVE
IN A LITTLE TOWN
Where the trees meet
across the street,
Where you wave your hand
and say "Hello"
To everyone you meet.
I like to stand for a moment
outside the grocery store
And listen to the friendly gossip
of the folks that live next door.
For life is interwoven
with the friends we learn to know,
And we hear their joys and sorrows
as we daily come and go.
So I like to live in a little town,
I care no more to roam,
For every house
in a little town
Is more than a house,
IT'S HOME.

Little Town is attributed to Pearl Wheatley, 1948.
Illustrator is anonymous.

This book is gratefully dedicated to my beloved parents, to all the Pagnis and Magnaghis, and to all who risked so much to journey to the New World for a better life, who were enriched and, in turn, enhanced their new country in so many ways.

And to Ed, Alexis, Luke, and Dean for your unconditional love, patience, encouragement, and support.

Contents

Acknowledgments

The genesis of Sweet Success is the result of wondering why my childhood in Crockett seemed idyllic and why I experienced the feeling of otherness when I left home. Don't most grow up in a community where just about everyone knows you and your entire family, where there are strong friendships, bonds, and a collective experience, and where the community shares your goals and dreams? I set off on an odyssey with this unease and willingness to search for answers. I encountered people who eagerly supported my efforts, and I am genuinely grateful for them. As I experienced the highs and lows of writing a book, I was nurtured, encouraged, and challenged to finish so that a story—our story—could be told.

Ed, my life partner, traveled the journey with me and always held my hand. Ed gave me the right amount of patience, encouragement, and support. He was my first reader and last editor and proofreader, and for that, I am grateful. Alexis, Luke, and Dean listened patiently, read, edited, gave me advice and constructive criticism, and pushed me when necessary.

Jim Marro, my editor, continually gave me the support I needed, whether by reading the entire manuscript and providing constructive criticism or suggesting further research. Jim started working with me to correct the passive voice in my writing more than twenty years ago. It appears Jim's job will never end.

Joe Fulcher provided early manuscript editing and encouragement and patiently edited all the photos and images shown throughout the book. Wanda Fulcher read the early chapters and encouraged me to continue.

Some of my Crockett family and friends graciously agreed to be interviewed. My cousins, Clarine Eramian and Ralph Pagni, helped me remember the details of our family's stories. Pam Pagni Sawyer, Dick Boyer, Diane Bottini Thomas, Fred Clerici, Marlena Airoldi, and Bea Auza were interviewed and shared their Crockett and Valona stories. At the same time, Ron Wilson shared his research on the Community Auditorium. So many asked about my progress and encouraged me. Cleo Protopapas met with me via Zoom during the early pandemic. Cleo encouraged me to dream about how I could tell this story. Jennifer Charvez read early chapters and provided valuable constructive criticism. Finally, Buzz Berryman, a high school friend whose friendship was rekindled at our 50th high school reunion, regularly emailed me his ideas, encouragement, and support.

The Crockett Historical Museum is a treasure trove of information. I wish to thank Erin Mullen Brosnan for her enthusiasm and guidance and Dick Boyer. Dick was always willing to drop whatever he was doing and help me find just the right image or piece of information I needed. Dick also verified details about life in Crockett and the refinery.

My community of writers and peers continually provided constructive criticism in an environment of trust and support. The University of California Berkeley Section Club Writers' Workshop and the UC Section Club Non-Fiction Writers' Group provided just that. Ann Huberty Duncan, Ione Elioff, Joanne Lagerstrom, Sally Stevens, Marilyn Vihman, and Elizabeth White read every chapter, provided suggested edits and advice, and challenged me to improve my writing and the manuscript. Susan Austin and Sally Tubach provided guidance, information, and mentorship as I searched for a publisher. Teresa De Luca Schooler, Lucia Falcone, and members of the UC Italian Section listened to my presentations, regularly checked on my progress, gave advice, and encouraged me to finish.

To all these and more, I am forever grateful.

Cover Painting, *Factory Town*
by Barse Miller,
Artist, 1946

Factory Town is used on the cover with permission from the family of Barse Miller.

Artist's Description of *Factory Town:*

"The painting "Factory Town" was painted in 1946 from a series of studies, including the watercolor "Sugar Mill" done at Crockett, California. This is one of the series on the themes of the Sacramento River, my project while on Guggenheim Fellowship.

Crockett, California is almost wholly supported by this sugar mill, the principal refinery for cane sugar operated by the California Hawaiian Sugar Corporation. The plant is picturesquely situated on the waterfront on the Carquinez Strait, which is here spanned by a bridge carrying toll rail and vehicular traffic between San Francisco and the Northwest.

Cargoes of raw sugar from the islands are here manufactured into finished goods and distributed nationally under the well-known C&H brand label.

Workers at the plant represent second and third generations of highly skilled labor. From the sociological standpoint, Crockett is a splendid example of American "factory town" managed with skill and benevolence by the "company" for the landowner workers at the plant. They have excellent primary and secondary schools, libraries, and a park system unusual for a town of this size population of about 4500.

The remaining factor in the obvious strata of social and financial importance of the residents whose houses rise in layers exactly contouring to the geographical character of the town—its richest representatives living in splendor on the crown of the steeply rising hills above the factory.

My compositional treatment of the scene is a greatly condensed design of the town. Its poetry is the organic heart and the beauty of its setting on the great waterway of the Sacramento."

Barse Miller, Artist

Introduction

They were right where Aunty Lou said they would be, in an old binder carefully stored in a musty newspaper-lined kitchen drawer in her old Victorian on Crockett's Fifth Avenue. Inside the binder were the coveted cake recipes she had collected and cherished during her long forty-five-year career at the California and Hawaiian Sugar Refining Company (C&H Sugar). The old binder was the first keepsake I brought home after my aunt died in December 2012.

At the end of her life, my aunt and I had many long conversations about her career at the refinery, life in Crockett and Valona, Crockett's immigrant neighborhood on the west side of town, friendships with her female colleagues, and the unique recipes they shared. In retrospect, these women were a bit like a secret culinary gang whose members enjoyed good food and friendships as they coped with the often-challenging work environment in the factory.

Over the years after my aunt's death, I kept returning to the recipes that had been so valuable to her. They seemed more than just a collection of cake recipes shared among women during their breaks in a refinery women's locker room. But what was their meaning, their significance, and why did they have such a strong emotional hold on me?

Having lived most of my life in Crockett and worked at the refinery for two summers while earning money to attend university, I had personal experiences and fond memories of my aunt's friends. They had supported and encouraged me to go to college and to seize every opportunity available, as the options offered me were not available to them in their day. Out of curiosity and perhaps appreciation, I wanted to learn more about Aunty Lou and her friends, their recipes, and the relevance and value of these recipes. I was inspired to document the stories of these women, which ultimately led to the creation of this book. I also understood that an essential element of Crockett's history would be forever lost if the stories of these working women weren't written and shared.

Thus, my journey began. Once committed to this task, work began in earnest. I started my research by sifting through several boxes of family artifacts in my attic, collected from Aunty Lou, my parents, and my aunts and uncles. I found family photos, artifacts, and pictures of Crockett, including several images of the working women at the refinery. I interviewed residents, some of whom had worked at the refinery, and continued my search at the Crockett Historical Museum and online. The museum houses a complete bound collection of *The Cubelet Press*, C&H Sugar's newsletter published from 1936 to 1992. Fortunately, the collection is digitized, making it easy to search its database. The *Cubelet Press* archive is a treasury of local Crockett history, documenting civic and family events, milestones, celebrations, births, and deaths. It became apparent that this bi-monthly newsletter was an essential element of C&H Sugar's corporate strategy. I found evidence that C&H Sugar's management had concluded early on that *The Cubelet Press* could educate its workforce and communicate the importance of the Company's corporate values and its role in the community. Everyone–the Company, employees, and unions–was urged to work together to benefit all. The stories of Crockett, Valona, and C&H Sugar's success and longevity are inspiring examples of what can be accomplished when people work together on a common purpose. In addition, this influential publication played a significant role in weaving together the fabric of the community and its tapestry. *The Cubelet Press* was essential in shaping the development of Crockett into a unique company town–in the best sense—by providing information, inspiration, and vision and by nurturing relationships and connections. Many of these relationships and connections still exist today among its past and present residents and even among former residents who have moved away, some throughout the country. Social media has kept these connections intact, bonds that have endured for generations.

The Crockett Historical Museum also has an extensive collection of photographs, displays, artifacts, cookbooks, personal recipe collections, and files on local history and town residents. Above all, the museum staff has a deep knowledge of local history and the refinery, which was essential to me.

Once my investigation was completed, I began writing. As I did so, it became apparent that I needed feedback and encouragement. After joining two writing groups and sharing my work with published writers, I was encouraged to include the history of Crockett and Valona in my story. My efforts and focus began to grow, and my initial plans of writing only about the working women at the refinery, whom I came to call the "Sisters," morphed into something much broader. To provide the context for my work, my efforts swelled to include how and why Crockett developed. This led me to draw several conclusions about life in Crockett during my Aunt Louise's and my lifetime, which are shared in this book. To describe the Italian immigrant experience shared by many Crockett residents, I have used the stories of my family, the Magnaghis and the Pagnis, and my father's, Faustino Pagni's, emigration to America. This work is included in Part 1 of the book.

Part 2 describes what it was like working in the refinery in the mid-1960s. These vignettes include meeting the working women at the refinery and packing sugar for the Vietnam War with other temporary summer hires bound for college. I also discuss what it was like working at various sugar production stations, including the Cube Station, Teabag Station, and Powder Mill. Interwoven throughout the book are stories about the refinery's working women.

Part 3 of the book is devoted to the vintage cake recipes in the collection. Processes such as developing a recipe timeline for the cakes, how recipes were tested, tasted, and photographed, and how methods are adjusted for today's bakers are discussed. For example, several recipes listed ingredients but omitted techniques, so these techniques had to be developed. Recipe terms were updated, and several products and measurements were adjusted. Baking notes and advice on baking a successful cake are also included. Since I have inherited and collected several Crockett community cookbooks, I researched and included what I learned about the genesis of these types of cookbooks in the United States.

Wherever possible, I added information about the authors of these recipes and my recollections of them. For privacy concerns, I have omitted names or used first names only. Perhaps this omission will trigger interesting conversations among readers and residents alike, causing some to wonder just who these bakers were.

In many ways, Crockett's story reveals a recipe for success. That is, how an industry leveraged its location, immigrants, and women to create a Golden Age in a quintessential California company town, a story similar to other small towns throughout the United States. In addition, the women working at the refinery were to the food industry what Rosie the Riveters were to World War II shipbuilding in Richmond, California. Like the Rosies, these women worked in industry when there weren't a lot of opportunities available to women, labor shortages were commonplace, and men were scarce. The women gathered at a specific time and place to do an essential job. At the same time, they nurtured their friendships, connections, and communities by contributing their talents, hard work, and energies to a collective effort. I stand on their shoulders; they are my heroes!

~

I hope you enjoy reading *Sweet Success*, reading about the history of Crockett, meeting the women, and perhaps baking a vintage cake. You may embark on a nostalgic journey. Like me, you may revisit memories of old friends and experiences, no matter where you live, for some of these stories and themes are universal to life in California and the United States in the twentieth century.

Part 1

The Creation of a Unique
Bay Area Community

Chapter One

Crockett's Distant Past

Driving east from San Francisco to Crockett along Interstate 80, through miles of sprawling urban growth, is to experience a megalopolis. The cities and communities of Oakland, Emeryville, Berkeley, El Cerrito, Richmond, El Sobrante, Pinole, Hercules, and Rodeo pass by as one approaches Crockett, the last offramp before the Carquinez Bridge. Travelers are lifted high on the elevated freeway as if flying over Valona, once Crockett's Italian immigrant community, and the Carquinez Straits. Below, the C&H Sugar Refinery, a massive, old multi-story brick structure built in 1881, with its vast warehouse and rusting seven stories high aqua-colored sugar bins, is a curiosity. The sugar bins, enormous silos, diminish in size towards Benicia like a study in perspective drawing.

Bay Area icons-the C&H Sugar Company Reginery and logo

It would be easy to assume Crockett is just another suburb of San Francisco if not for this relic of the past with the refinery's universally known C&H Sugar logo. Because of Crockett's small size, it is easy to suppose that its history must be insignificant. But nestled between the rolling hills and shores of the Carquinez Straits, Crockett has a rich story to reveal as an isolated and independent community, first inhabited by California indigenous people, the Karkins, an Ohlone tribe, by the Spanish and the Mexicans, and finally by European settlers. Immigrants flooded Crockett from Europe and Mexico, and migrants from the Dust Bowl. Crockett's history is rooted in its indigenous people's story and the diversity of its settlers, men and women, who provided the labor for its shipping industry and industrial development.

Despite its location in the San Francisco megalopolis, Crockett remains a geographically isolated community framed on all sides by its steep hills, open land zoned for farming, managed by the East Bay Regional Parks District, and the waters of the straits.

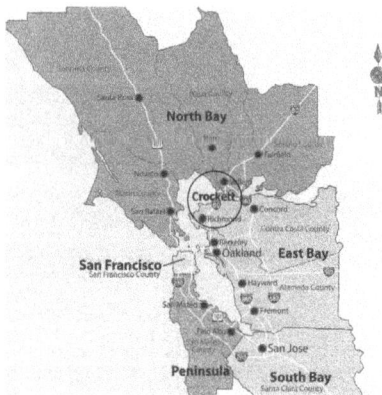

A map of the San Francisco Bay Area shows Crockett's location northeast of San Francisco

24

To fully understand Crockett's evolution and the influences that affected those working at the refinery, it is essential to know about Crockett's distant past and its history of isolation. This isolation was followed by rapid shipping and industrial growth and worker shortages, which were catalysts for bringing immigrants to Crockett's shores, resulting in its rich ethnic, gender, and socioeconomic diversity.

Crockett's indigenous inhabitants, the Karkins, were named by the Commandante at the Presidio of Monterey from a Greek word meaning "crab." Likely, the Commandante chose this name because of the abundance of small crabs in the straits. Also called *Los Carquines* in Spanish, the Karkins were one of eight Ohlone indigenous peoples living in the region that made their home in Crockett's hills and fertile valley. In 1772, Pedro Fages, a Spanish explorer, encountered the peaceful and friendly Karkins. The Karkins were hunters and gatherers who settled here, finding an abundant food supply in the hills, straits, and fresh water found in the valley. With bows and arrows, the Karkins killed large and small game. They hunted birds, including quail, wild ducks, geese, pelicans, and white and gray cranes. Elk, wild cattle, deer, antelope, coyote, mountain lions, grizzly bears, wildcats, hares, and rabbits were hunted in the hills. They fished in the Carquinez Straits' waterways with canoes made of tule reeds, and nets and enjoyed salmon, bass, trout, sturgeon, mussels, clams, and crab. The Karkins gathered roots and bulbs, berries, and acorns from the hundreds of oak trees abundant on Crockett's steep grassy hills.

The Karkins built a sacred shellmound, a burial site, and a longhouse on the grounds of what is now the Old Homestead, Crockett's first European settler home. Shellmounds

Tule canoes were the Karkin's mode of transportation

were formed from mounds of discarded organic matter and earth over thousands of years. The shells came from abundant crustaceans and mollusks found in the straits. Shellmounds were located near freshwater streams. They served as a gathering place for ceremonies and feasts, where families lived and worked together throughout the year. The local freshwater stream, fed by several springs in the surrounding hillsides, rushed downhill to join the Carquinez Straits' salty tidal waters. This valley stream and the springs that supply it still exist today, although much of its flow is buried in a culvert under the Carquinez Middle School and John Swett High School. The stream is visible again on the west side of the Old Homestead garden and often overflows its banks in a heavy rainstorm. With California's mild weather and their creativity and resourcefulness, the

Karkins had everything they needed to live a stable, comfortable life.

Karkins wove baskets to store acorns found in the hills

The Karkins' lives were catastrophically disrupted in 1776 after Father Junipero Serra established Mission Dolores in San Francisco. The Spaniards captured the Karkins and transported them to the mission, where they were imprisoned. They were forced to work as slaves on the mission's farms and agricultural fields. Those who rebelled and escaped were hunted down and returned to the Mission by Spanish soldiers quartered at the Presidio. Many Karkins died from imprisonment, extremely unbearable working conditions, contracting European-borne diseases, and depression. The Karkins never returned home, no longer living peacefully in Crockett's valley or along its shores.

The missions prospered in California until the Mexican Revolution in 1823. With a new Mexican government in power, land grants were offered to reward loyal Mexicans, and the missions lost their influence and holdings. Ignacio M. Martinez received a land grant in 1842 of 18,000 acres, which he named Rancho Pinole. It ran from Point Pinole to what is now the city of Martinez. The land grant included all of Crockett's hills and valleys. Don Martinez was a cattle rancher whose livestock drank from Crockett's springs and streams that had once sustained the Karkins. There were no fences in the hills, so the Mexican Vaqueros, horsemen whose skills and traditions were the foundation for American cowboys, herded and drove Martinez's cattle, Texas Longhorns, to slaughter. Their hides and tallow were shipped by boat to San Francisco.

Mexican Vaqueros roamed the hills of Crockett, managing Ignacio M. Martinez's Texas longhorn cattle

By 1840, ships were using the deep channel passage of the Carquinez Straits to reach central California. After gold was discovered in 1848, miners and entrepreneurs began sailing from San Francisco to Stockton and Sacramento, increasing boat traffic up the Carquinez Straits. Various types of watercraft, such as ferries, riverboats, and small barges, passed by Crockett transporting supplies and equipment for use in California mines or on farms sprouting up in the Sacramento and San Joaquin River Valleys. In 1850, the city of Martinez, located ten miles east of what is now Crockett, became the county seat for both Alameda and Contra Costa Counties. In 1853, Benicia became the State Capitol but remained so for only thirteen months.

Judge Joseph Bryant Crockett

In 1865, Judge Joseph Bryant Crockett, an attorney and eventually a California Supreme Court associate justice, settled a long and often bitter legal case for Teodora Soto, a wealthy landowner who owned a portion of what is now Contra Costa County. The name of this land grant was the

Rancho del Hambre y las Bolsas, which extended northwest from Martinez to Lafayette, California. The courts litigated the case over rights and boundaries within the rancho. For his fee in settling the case, Judge Crockett received a plot of land along the Carquinez Straits. This land eventually became the town of Crockett. Judge Crockett was concerned about protecting his property from squatters prevalent in the Arroyo del Hambre, the name of the Mexican land grant in the region. The land grant was named the "valley of hunger" because a group of Mexicans had run out of food while camping in the area years before, ironically in a place where the Karkins had once found an abundant food supply. Judge Crockett asked Thomas Edwards, a friend, to settle on his land and protect it from squatters. Judge Crockett had met Edwards, a pioneer farmer, while Edwards worked as a mate on steamers on the Mississippi River. Edwards and his wife, Mary Pugh Edwards, both born in Wales and with six children, accepted the offer.

Thomas Edwards,
as a young man

The Edwards family were risk-takers and no strangers to hard work. Thomas had been at sea for ten years. Mary had traveled to America independently with a group of women who each sought to find a husband in America. After their marriage, the Edwards settled in St. Louis. In 1850, they traveled by covered wagon to California. After stopping to rest their horse team, they accomplished the last part of the journey alone. Mary and Thomas settled in the southeastern Sierra Nevada mountains in Independence, California.

After accepting Judge Crockett's offer in 1865, the Edwards family left Independence, traveled by wagon, and sailed by riverboat to Benicia. From Benicia, they ferried to Bull Valley, now known as Port Costa, just three miles east of Crockett. Judge Crockett had been wise to be concerned about squatters on his property. A group of woodchoppers squatting on the Judge's land prevented the Edwards family from moving to Crockett for a year. While waiting to move to Crockett, the Edwards spent 1866 in a small cabin at Bull Valley, raising chickens and dairy cows and marketing their farm products in Martinez and Benicia.

Eventually, the woodchoppers moved on and abandoned their tiny home in Crockett. The Edwards family then moved into the small abandoned cabin. Soon after, the woodchoppers returned to the cabin, threatening a fight. Bernardo Fernandez, a Portuguese immigrant, pioneer of Pinole, and owner of extensive landholdings in Contra Costa County, intervened and stopped a band of sixteen men from killing the Edwards family. Mr. Fernandez convinced the men that Edwards had title to the land, so they left without a fight.

Finally settling on Judge Crockett's land, the Edwards family located their homestead on the shoreline of the Carquinez Straits in Crockett's valley, adjacent to the same stream and freshwater supply the Karkins had found so

The Old Homestead, as it was in the late 1800s,
was located on the shores of the Carquinez Straits

valuable. When the foundation for the Edwards home, today known as The Old Homestead, was excavated, the remains of a Karkin were discovered. According to local legend, the remains were found in what appeared to be a seated position. However, today, it is known that the remains would have been arranged in the fetal position, a common Ohlone ritual burial practice. The Edwards had stumbled upon the shellmound and sacred burial grounds abandoned by the Karkins almost a century before. By the end of 1867, the Edwards family had built a house, barn, and dock over a shallow part of the bay that led to deeper water. Here, they moored their sailboat, the "Plowboy," and sailed it on the waters of the Carquinez Straits to transport their garden products, eggs, and milk to markets in the area.

While many people came to California searching for gold in the Sierra Nevada Mountain Range in the 1850s, most gold miners failed to find enough gold to sustain themselves. However, some were entrepreneurs, foresaw commercial opportunities amongst the miners in the gold mining towns, and began to make their wealth. For example, Levi Strauss made his fortune selling dry goods and clothing. He helped develop jeans, durable work pants meant to withstand the harsh working conditions of the Gold Rush. Dominico Ghirardelli, a chocolatier from Rapallo, a city near Genoa, Italy, sold dry goods and chocolate. William Fargo and Henry Wells established banks in rural areas of California. Many others succeeded by farming wheat, barley, and oats in the fertile valleys of the Sacramento and San Joaquin Rivers. California had imported wheat until 1854 but soon became a significant grain exporter. California wheat was known worldwide as a clean, plump, dry, weighty grain. Because it was dry, it didn't mold in shipment and could be held in bulk storage for long periods. California wheat earned higher prices in England and France because when ground into flour, it absorbed much more water in bread baking than other types of flour. This resulted in more weight to the loaf for each pound of flour used, an obvious benefit to bakers. Crockett's future became intricately tied to these grains.

Grain warehouses on the shores of the Carquinez Straits

By 1876, with the railroad's continuous development and the need to move and ship grain to other markets worldwide, many shipping docks were built that stretched from Crockett to Port Costa. Crockett was known as Wheatville. By 1881, the region became the center for storing and shipping California-grown wheat, overtaking San Francisco and Oakland in tonnage shipped. Tall sailing ships, both schooners and clipper ships, anchored and docked in the Carquinez Straits' deep waters, awaiting their turn to be loaded. The ships were primarily schooners built to carry cargo in their holds. By contrast, Clipper ships built for speed and meant to "clip" time from the length of their voyages weren't as prevalent on the straits. Clipper ships sailed out of San Francisco and moved more valuable, smaller cargo, called "niche" cargo, such as tea, gold from California mines, and passengers.

*Grain sailing ships that transported grains
from the Carquinez Straits internationally*

Workers loaded tons of California's grain on board the vessels before sailing around the horn to East Coast cities and Europe. Voyages lasted 100 to 260 days. Trans-Pacific ships carried wheat to China, Japan, and the South Seas. Ships that arrived in California were laden with supplies and left with a hull full of California grains. A booming grain business ensued, and brisk international trade developed. Eventually, a ferry connected Bull Valley (Port Costa) to Benicia, enabling grain to be transported across the straits and then by rail to Sacramento.

The region became one of the leading grain shipping ports globally. By 1880, over a third of the ships leaving San Francisco for foreign ports had been loaded with wheat on the Carquinez Straits. In 1883, as many as 500 rails cars of grain arrived daily for distribution, and by January 1895, more than 259,000 tons of wheat were stored along the straits. In the 1890s, grain warehouses stretching from Port Costa to Crockett to Point Pinole shipped more than one million tons yearly. In December 1895, nineteen ships were docked for loading while eight others waited for wharf space.

In the 1950s, it was still possible to drive the winding "old road" between Crockett and Martinez and see spectacular views of the straits and the dark brown hulls of three tall ships, schooners, their masts still intact. The vessels were ghostlike, particularly in the fog, and the sight could stimulate over-active imaginations. The tall ships floated eerily and rolled with large swells at high tide, and it was easy to imagine pirates or spirits on board. At low tide, the tall-masted ships sank back into the mud. Over the ensuing years, the vessels decayed and are no longer visible today. However, in 2024, it is still possible to see, at low tide, the

184-foot skeleton of the shipwrecked "Forester" on the shores of the Radke Martinez Regional Shoreline Park in Martinez. The Forester was a lumber schooner built in 1900 in Alameda at the Hay and Wright Shipyard.

The Garden City Ferry's rusting hulk can also be seen along the Carquinez Straits' shores at Crockett's east end. Built in 1879 in San Francisco under the direction of W. E. Collyer for $120,000 ($3,723,912 in 2024 dollars) and named for the City of San Jose, the Garden City was a paddlewheel steamboat that plowed bay waters until her retirement in 1929. Built for the South Pacific Coast Railroad Company, the Garden City first worked between Alameda and San Francisco and was later assigned to the bay's "Creek Route" until retirement. In the 1800s, "The Creek" referred to the Oakland Estuary, an inlet of San Francisco Bay. It included Oakland's ferry landing site, where Jack London Square is located today at the foot of Broadway, and Lake Merritt. The Garden City was built of wood as an oil-burning side-wheeler, 243 feet long, sixty-six feet wide over the guardrails, and fifteen feet deep at the hull's center. She carried passengers by day and freight by night, with a seating capacity of 721 passengers and space for forty-five automobiles. Imagining the giant paddle wheels' size at twenty-three and one-half feet in diameter gives a good picture of the size of the ferry itself.

The Garden City had a well-earned reputation and received many honors. Known as "The Presidents' Ferryboat," she rendezvoused just outside the Golden Gate with the ship carrying former President Ulysses S. Grant when he returned from a post-presidency world tour that included stops in Japan and China. The ferry also carried Presidents Hayes, McKinley, Teddy Roosevelt, and President Wilson.

The Garden City Ferry once transported
U.S. presidents and international royalty

The Garden City ferried several sovereigns, including King Gustav of Sweden in 1915, to the Pan-Pacific Exposition in San Francisco. King Albert and Queen Elizabeth of Belgium were on board with their royal party on October 14, 1919, and received a battleship gun salute. In 1926, the Garden City carried the Crown Prince and Princess of Sweden. The Garden City's tenure on the bay was full of excitement, adventures, and escapades, including fights, rescues, deaths, and sailing mishaps. The most notable of these was a near-miss collision with a wooden schooner.

The largest single group of passengers to board the Garden City was Coxey's Army, which stormed over the railroad and ferry guards in San Francisco on February 1894 to board the ferry. The Global Panic and Stock Market crash of

1893 caused increased unemployment in the United States. In response, Jacob Coxey organized a march from Ohio to the U.S. Capitol in Washington, D.C., to convince lawmakers to put the unemployed to work fixing the nation's dilapidated roadways. Ultimately, the debate was over the government's responsibility to provide employment for its citizens. A group of Californians planning to join Coxey's army boarded the Garden City for the march on Washington. It is said that on board that day was Jack London, California's novelist, journalist, and social activist. The Garden City's owners decided it was cheaper to let the migrant army ride than try to have them arrested for non-payment of fare and the food consumed by this motley crew. Coxey's army and protest disbanded on the shores of the Mississippi River and never reached Washington, D.C.

The Garden City Ferry at Eckley's Resort

CHAPTER 1

In 1934, local businessman Michael Hallissy purchased the Garden City. One of the refinery's tugs towed the ferry to Eckley, a growing resort Mr. Hallissy owned on the straits between Crockett and Port Costa. The Garden City's sea valves were flooded, and the ferry came to rest in the mud-flats close to shore. Mr. Hallisy remodeled the ferry to accommodate a residence, the largest dance floor in Contra Costa County, and a headquarters for a sport fishing business. The headquarters included a lunch counter, a bar, a tackle shop, and rooms for fishermen.

In the summer, Crockett residents could enjoy a sweet, bubbly 7UP for the kids or a beer for the adults while sitting on the deck of the Garden City. The brisk cooling breeze off the straits and the ice-cold drink combined perfectly for Crockett's hot, sweltering summer days. Little did these visitors know they were visiting a hard-working, grand lady of San Francisco Bay waters with an illustrious, storied past. In August 1983, the Garden City, an essential part of California's rich maritime history, was reduced to smoke, ash, and mangled metal. Crockett's residents watched helplessly as flames from an arson-caused wildfire spread rapidly between Crockett and Port Costa. The fire consumed the Garden City, an aged ferry pier, and an abandoned train platform. Today, only the Garden City's boilers and paddlewheel hub remain above the waterline about fifty feet from shore.

As the shipping industry expanded, unemployed railroad men, longshoremen, warehousemen, sailors, and immigrants roamed Crockett's streets, looking for work, housing, and amenities. Because there was no housing, the working men slept the night between work shifts wherever they could find a safe place to lie down. When their work assignments were finished, they traveled to San Francisco for amusement and diversion until they were needed back at the docks in Crockett. It was a rough period for Crockett and its workers. Saloons lined the streets, and bars provided lively refuge and entertainment between work hours and sleep. Many of these bars were still in business in the late 1970s.

Men such as these walked the streets
of Crockett looking for work

Thomas Edwards, who by 1878 was a wealthy man, witnessed the development of a rail line in front of his home and along the waterfront and realized his chance to develop the area into a town. He bought Judge Crockett's property for $30,000, naming his new village after his friend, the Judge. Within a year, Edwards sold land rights to Abraham Dubois Starr, who built a flour mill, the largest on the West Coast. The old mill now houses the C&H Sugar Refinery. Edwards also sold a hill west of his valley to Dr. John Strentzel, a Polish immigrant, physician, and pioneer in

California experimental horticulture. This hill was developed into the village of Valona. It's worth noting that Dr. Strentzel was John Muir's father-in-law.

Crockett was on the move and became a bustling place. The Edwards brothers expanded their business and opened a store. On March 3, 1882, J.L. Heald opened his Agricultural Works, a foundry that was the county's most extensive company of its kind. The Pinkerton House was built in 1881 to house local workers, and the Starr Hotel followed. The Carquinez Grammar School opened in 1882, and Crockett's first Presbyterian Church service was held at the school on April 15, 1883. On June 15, 1883, Crockett's Post Office was established. By 1896, Crockett had a newspaper – *The Record*, and the *Crockett Signal* followed in 1899. In 1908, the Crockett Branch of the Bank of Pinole opened its doors. John Swett High School opened in 1927 and was named after John Swett, considered the "father of the California public school system." By 1931, the district served close to one thousand students. Many of these students were immigrants, and English was their second language.

The Crockett Lumber Company on the shores of the Carquinez Straits

New arrivals had learned about Crockett's job opportunities by word-of-mouth or through letters sent home by friends and family already working here. Eager to establish a new life in Crockett and Valona, new residents began to build their homes. As small as Crockett was, it was divided into three townships. The town of Crockett extended from West Street east; Crolona, whose name combined Crockett and Valona, from West Street to Third Avenue, and Valona from Third Avenue west. Crockett and Valona are still noted as townships in California, while Crolona is not. Crolona was merely a zone of land owned by C&H Sugar, where the company built many town amenities and executive homes.

Northern Europeans, such as the Irish, English, Welch, and Germans, tended to settle on the east side of town because they had arrived earlier. Settlers from Mediterranean countries, such as Italy, Greece, Spain, France, and Portugal, established their homes on Crockett's west side, in Valona, near family and friends. Their native languages, including dialects specific to their regions or villages, were spoken here. Other settlers came from Mexico and America's heartland as Dust Bowl survivors. All these new settlers were working-class people looking for employment. Today, at Crockett's only stoplight, the handsome, unusual clock in the downtown plaza has two names. Looking east, the clock face says, "Crockett." Looking west from Second Avenue, the face of the clock says, "Valona," the Italian immigrant neighborhood.

The Global Panic and Stock Market crash of 1893 that catalyzed Coxey's Army's formation to protest socioeconomic conditions in the United States decimated the grain business. The decline in California wheat production was hastened by the development of diversified farming, including orchard crops. National and international markets, including Argentina, Canada, and the Northwest, entered the grain business. The flour mill closed in 1893. George W. McNear, Sr., bought the vacant flour mill in 1894 and began to refine sugar beets. Simultaneously, sugar cane growers in Hawaii, looking for a facility to process their sugar cane on the mainland, struck a deal with McNear. On November 30, 1897, the California Beet Sugar and Refining Company purchased the Starr Mill, including the Edwards ranch. The refinery was modified by Robert P. Rithet, George W. McNear, C. W. Cooke, and others to process beets and sugar cane. The sugar mill started operations in the Spring of 1898. At first, the supply of raw materials, sugar beets, and cane was intermittent and insufficient to make the refinery profitable. Eventually, McNear leased the business to Claude Spreckels, who significantly impacted the U.S. sugar industry. With the supply of sugar from Hawaii expanding and stabilizing, the refinery became steadily profitable, making it the vital asset it is today to California and the San Francisco Bay Area.

The refinery's name was changed to California and Hawaiian Sugar Refining Company. At 10:00 a.m. on March 10, 1906, the American flag was hoisted at the refinery. The C&H Sugar steam whistle, joined by train and boat whistles, blew vigorously, announcing the start of operations at the refinery. Business was booming. At one time, C&H Sugar was owned by thirty-three of the fifty-two Hawaiian sugar plantations and refined 80% of Hawaii's sugar production. The refinery remained in Crockett due to its location, that is, its proximity to San Francisco, access to deep water and rail facilities, 3,000-foot frontage on the straits, and deepwater docks. In 1906, Claude Spreckels handed over the reins of managing the refinery to George Morrison Rolph, who was instrumental in developing C&H Sugar into today's American industrial legend.

Crockett continued to grow. Still isolated due to a lack of roads, by 1920, Crockett and neighboring Valona were busy, self-sustaining small towns. The town's name officially remained "Crockett" because the refinery, the post office, and the train depot were in that part of town. Crockett and Valona developed into two communities due to the area's robust employment opportunities and fair wages. Crockett and Valona offered duplicate services to residents, such as schools, banks, stores, theaters, funeral parlors, businesses, and fire departments. There was an intense rivalry between the two small towns that would continue into the twentieth century. In 1926, the two fire departments agreed to cooperate and assist each other in the event of a second-alarm fire.

~

The absence of a loyal, steady workforce to meet the growing sugar industry demand would threaten to restrain C&H Sugar's growth and Crockett's development. Worker recruitment and retention in a geographically isolated rural town had to be solved. Under George Morrison Rolph's leadership, alleviating this risk would be fundamental to Rolph's and C&H Sugar's success. Eventually, C&H Sugar's progressive industrial relations programs would also catapult Crockett into its Golden Age, making it a unique and extraordinary place to live.

Chapter Two

Crockett Becomes a Company Town

To truly grasp Crockett's essence, one must explore the Italian word *benessere*, 'well-being,' as it perfectly captures a foundational element of the management strategy for developing C&H Sugar and Crockett itself. It's crucial to understand what *Benessere* was, who introduced it, when it came about, and why. Even though it is doubtful the Company knew the Italian word for this industrial relations strategy, management implemented the concept in tangible and consequential ways. Like the amenities and benefits many technology companies offer in the 21st century to recruit and retain a stable workforce, C&H Sugar created a balanced work and community environment, consistently concerned with employee and family welfare. The company offered liveable wages, affordable housing, security, health, safety, and an engaging community life. Above all, this strategy is evident in the relationship between C&H Sugar and Crockett itself, fostering a strong sense of community that resonates even today.

Whatever it might have been called, Italian immigrant families certainly would have discussed the concept and its benefits in the context of their new lives in Crockett and Valona and the opportunities available to them. These opportunities weren't available in Italy, and immigrants, with their unwavering resilience, were willing to risk everything to acquire them to benefit their families. After a long Sunday or holiday lunch, when the weather was warm and comfortable, it was common for Italian families to sit outside in the

SWEET SUCCESS

garden or on the front porch. Family elders, the storytellers, would tell and retell meaningful family stories during these special moments. Children had their favorite stories and often asked the elders to retell them, listening intently as the family's oral history came to life. The most important tales would have been about the family's life in Italy and their complicated but necessary decision to emigrate to America. These were stories of the old country: *miseria*, 'poverty,' the perils of fascism, food scarcity, faith, courage, heartache, risk, adventure, and hard work. The elders understood the power and significance of these stories, which were meant to enchant, teach, and inspire the next generations, children and young adults, to succeed in America, their new country, against all odds.

Benessere was conceived and implemented under the leadership of George Morrison Rolph, the first Plant Manager of C&H Sugar. Mr. Rolph directed refinery operations from 1906 until 1914 when he transferred to the San Francisco office as corporation president. He was President of the company until 1920, when he became Chairman of the Board. Mr. Rolph faced the daunting challenge of recruiting and retaining a stable, loyal workforce in a geographically isolated town where many citizens were immigrants, first-generation immigrant children, or transplants from other areas of the United States.

With Mr. Rolph at the helm, C&H Sugar developed a unique progressive strategy that was persistent and committed to creating a strong, mutually beneficial partnership between itself, the industry, its employees, and its setting, Crockett. This pervasive strategy created a much-needed loyal, productive, dedicated workforce and ultimately handsome profits for the corporation. In the best sense, it also developed Crockett into the essence of an early

46

twentieth-century industrial company town. Crockett was a hybrid company town because its citizens, not the company, owned most homes. For Crockett's children, it meant enjoying what seemed to be an idyllic childhood in Crockett's Golden Age that lasted for several decades.

George Morrison Rolph

George Morrison Rolph was born in San Francisco on February 6, 1873, the third son of his San Francisco pioneer parents, James and Margaret Nicol Rolph. The Rolphs had emigrated to the United States from London, England, in 1858. They settled in the Mission District of San Francisco. George's father, James, was associated with the Bank of California his entire career. His mother, Margaret, bore six children. Mr. Rolph's brother, James Rolph, Jr., also known as "Sunny Jim," was the Mayor of San Francisco for an unprecedented nineteen years, from 1911 to 1930. He was also a Depression-era governor of California from 1931 to 1934.

George Morrison Rolph attended San Francisco public schools in the Mission District. He earned enough money to put himself through Stanford University by selling newspapers. Even as a young boy, he had good business sense. At one time, his newspaper business had over 600 customers. Mr. Rolph and Herbert Hoover, who would become the thirty-first president of the United States from 1929 to 1933, were classmates and friends at Stanford. Their friendship endured over the years, resulting in Mr. Hoover offering Rolph several career opportunities.

After graduating from Stanford University, Mr. Rolph worked at Risdon Iron Works in San Francisco and a lumber mill in Fresno County. Rolph's career in the sugar industry began in 1903 when he traveled to the Hawaiian Islands, where he studied the cultivation and refining of sugar cane into raw sugar. Working for the Alexander and Baldwin Company in the clerical department, Rolph soon advanced to a junior executive position and returned to California in 1905. In 1906, Mr. Rolph assumed the management of the newly formed California and Hawaiian Sugar Refining Company in Crockett after millions of dollars had been spent repurposing the factory from grain milling to sugar refining.

At the beginning of World War I, George Morrison Rolph left C&H Sugar for two years to assume a federal government position. President Woodrow Wilson created the United States Food Administration to exert government power over food to help win the war. By the time the United States entered the war in April 1917, this action was necessary because food reserves in the United States had been exhausted by Europe's demand for food. American farmers needed at least an entire growing season to replenish these reserves. The necessity was to ship food overseas to supply American soldiers and allies. Under the auspices of Executive Order 2679-A, Rolph's friend, Herbert Hoover, led the Food Administration Department for two years. The department managed the food supply, distribution, and conservation, facilitated transportation, and prevented monopolies and hoarding. The Executive Order also created a robust advertising campaign asking Americans to conserve food by eating less. Mr. Hoover appointed Rolph to the Sugar Division and later made him the Sugar Equalization Board chairman. An accomplished, effective leader and manager, Mr. Rolph saved a surplus of $30,000,000 ($671,706,569 in 2024 dollars) through efficiencies. He returned this surplus to the United States Treasury when his tenure ended at the war's end.

1917 was a busy year for Mr. Rolph, who wrote a book published in San Francisco that is still available today. Titled *Something about Sugar: Its History, Growth, Manufacture, and Distribution*, it documented the history of sugar, its production in different parts of the world, the various steps by which sugar is made from sugar cane and beets, and how sugar is prepared for the consumer. On the title page, Mr. Rolph wrote that "sugar is nothing more nor less than concentrated sunshine."

George Morrison Rolph was a prominent San Francisco club man. He and Herbert Hoover were members of the Bohemian Club, an elite, private, invitation-only, gentleman-only club whose membership was open only to Caucasians and non-Jews. The Bohemian Club was founded in San Francisco in 1872 by a group of male artists, writers, and journalists interested in arts and culture. Membership in the club expanded to include successful, affluent businessmen, politicians, and prominent men known worldwide. Notable

Bohemian Club members include Bret Harte, Mark Twain, Jack London, Richard Nixon, Ronald Regan, Henry Kissinger, Clint Eastwood, and Walter Cronkite.

The club hosts a two-week July retreat at their 2,700-acre campground, the Bohemian Grove, in Monte Rio, in Northern California's Sonoma County. The club's influential, politically conservative, rich, and famous members leave their corporate worries behind to enjoy high-level conversations, the outdoors, music, and theater. Business conversations aren't allowed at the Grove. The only exception to this policy was in 1942 when planning for the Manhattan Project, the effort that produced the first nuclear weapons instrumental in ending World War II, took place at the Grove.

George Morrison Rolph was a California and Bay Area native son and *bon vivant*. Surmising that Rolph was strongly inspired by his upbringing in San Francisco, his Stanford University education, his brother James' political career, and the Bohemian Club, it is easy to conclude that these influenced the growth of C&H Sugar and the town of Crockett. When Rolph came to Crockett in the early 20th century, Crockett was a remote, rough-and-tumble, semi-rural, isolated small town. Perhaps Rolph understood that if he had to live in Crockett, not San Francisco, he would indulge his interests and passions, the arts and culture, by infusing them into his new hometown, and everyone benefitted. Perhaps unknowingly, he embedded a piece of himself into Crockett's master planning, brick-and-mortar structures, and the hearts and minds of its citizens.

While delivering much-needed economic growth to the region, Rolph's unique progressive management strategy promised a secure future for C&H Sugar employees and Crockett's citizens, enabling them to develop well-balanced lives. Key to the program's success was an informed understanding between the company and its employees, collaboration, and confidence. Its goal was labor stabilization, improved production, quality, service, and reduced costs. The strategy was based on the concept that an employee has six prime interests: 1) a good, liveable annual income; 2) job security; 3) insurance for earnings, sickness, and disability; 4) the absence of arbitrary management practices; 5) access to reasonable and inexpensive housing; and 6) an exciting community life. Mr. Rolph once said of his progressive program, "We do it because it is good business and because it produces our sugar cheaper and better."

Services to employees were generous, providing medical, hospital, and disability insurance, legal advice, aid for those yet to become citizens, and Americanization classes for aliens. Restrooms and smoking quarters, programs promoting living within one's means, savings plans, lost and found programs, Christmas bonuses, and a pension at retirement were also offered. Safety at the refinery and around Crockett was embedded in the culture, and the company provided plant protection, gatekeepers, and watchmen. Recreation and amusements around town were legendary, including parks, playgrounds, company gardens, and company greenhouses. There was also an extensive continuing education program for adults at John Swett High School.

The company enabled its employees to own a home and enjoy abundant amenities, ample leisure time, and accessibility to the arts and culture. Happy employees committed to happy home lives became a core value for the company and Crockett. This concept of *Benessere* was a central factor, making Crockett a unique place to live. Equally crucial to Rolph's strategy was organized labor's vital contribution.

Its power and support were a continual check and balance on the Company, enabling workers to earn a fair wage and putting employees on a path of upward economic mobility. Rolph's progressive influence on Crockett's development into the community it is today cannot be over-emphasized.

In 1914, a labor shortage threatened, and Mr. Rolph took extraordinary measures to continue his efforts to recruit and retain a steady workforce. He reduced employee workdays from ten or twelve hours per day to eight hours per day and did so without lowering employee wages. Employees worked less while receiving the same compensation. The employee wage scale was said to be the best in the industry. A game-changer for the citizens of Crockett, Mr. Rolph demonstrated to the Board of Directors that the reduced hours didn't impact the refinery's profitability. He encouraged the Board and stockholders to continue the policy. This new work-life balance stirred refinery employees' loyalty, who were productive in gratitude for their increased leisure time.

Hotel Crockett on Loring Avenue

Mr. Rolph initially found living conditions in Crockett deplorable–substandard from the standpoints of availability, comfort, convenience, sanitation, and health. A large hotel, Hotel Crockett, offering approximately 170 rooms, had opened on Loring Avenue near the refinery in 1898 but could not provide sufficient housing for all workers in the area. C&H Sugar continued to remodel and expand the hotel. When the hotel reached capacity at 280 rooms, temporary tent structures were built behind the hotel, and the company ran a hotel business at an annual loss to house employees. Rolph realized he needed to do even more to provide much-needed housing and stabilize the workforce. His answer was the Home Building Program, which constructed homes on company-owned land. The program also developed a health and sanitation infrastructure to support the new homes, including utilities, streets, sidewalks, garbage collection service, sewers, and a permanent sanitary commission for the town. By 1920, 163 houses were built. 74 percent of these new homes were built for employees with financial assistance from the company; 14 percent were built for employees without financial aid; and 12 percent were constructed by non-employees on company lots procured with financial company assistance.

The program continued through 1927, when an additional seventeen homes were built. In addition, C&H Sugar partnered with local banks to provide affordable mortgages with small down payments and reasonable monthly payments. The standard was small two-bedroom, one-bathroom cottages of about 800 square feet, called sugar shacks. These small cottages still line Cooke and Atherton Avenues, just off Pomona Street, in Crockett's Tenney Terrace neighborhood. Tenney Terrace was named for Vernon Tenney, a

Tenney Terrace built by C&H
Sugar's Home Building Program

well-connected C&H Sugar executive. Mr. Tenney's father was the President and Manager of Castle & Cooke, Ltd., a real estate development and investment company founded in Hawaii in 1851. He was also the President of the Matson Navigation Co., which transported raw cane sugar from Hawaii to the Crockett refinery for decades.

In the ensuing years, C&H Sugar continued its aggressive building program, intending to create a model community. The large hill southeast of the refinery, also known as Company Hill, became home to executives who lived in beautiful multi-story shingled homes and cottages. Many were designed in the same Arts and Crafts architectural style found in the Berkeley Hills and Maui, Hawaii, where sugar cane was grown and shipped across the Pacific Ocean to C&H Sugar's dock.

Construction began on Rolph's home, known as The Company House, in April 1917 and was completed by the end of that year. The *Crockett Signal*, one of Crockett's several newspapers at the time, noted on March 23, 1917, that the house would be constructed in a colonial design, two stories high, fully furnished, and modern in every way. When work began on his home, Rolph lived in Washington, D.C., working for Herbert Hoover as the Sugar Commission Head. After World War I, Rolph returned to Crockett and lived in the home until just before he died in 1932.

Mr. Rolph's house, built on the crest of the hill, had a grand covered portico. Its grounds had a beautifully landscaped turnaround with a stately flagpole. Below the house was the C&H Sugar logo, annually planted with bright, colorful flowers. It prominently stood out on a slope devoid of trees. In 1923, the *Honolulu Advertiser* noted that the hill was a botanical garden with ambitious "homes dotting the thirty-degree slopes." Adjacent to the house was a two-room cottage aptly called the Guest Cottage. It was designed to house Hawaiian visitors and make them feel at home when they visited the refinery. The Guest Cottage had an extended lanai; all its furnishings were wicker island pieces with Hawaiian floral upholstery.

*C&H Sugar's Company House, the former
home of George Morrison Rolph and his family*

After the Rolphs left the residence in 1932, the Company House was converted for C&H Sugar's Management and Board functions, and it accommodated notable visitors to the refinery. The Guest Cottage provided the venue for company and community awards dinners, such as the company's service awards. C&H Sugar sold the Company House and Guest House to a private owner in August 2000.

The Crockett Club, as seen from Rolph Park Drive

Continuing their aggressive building program and providing much-needed recreation and amenities for residents, in 1916, C&H Sugar built the Crockett Club. The YMCA initially managed the club, but the company terminated the arrangement because it didn't allow athletic facilities to be open on Sundays. C&H Sugar then employed the club's management team. Initially a men's club, it was erected in the same style as the executive houses. The symmetrical entrance to the club was grand and set back from the street, and park benches lined the covered portico. The central wooden revolving door was the entry highlight, replete with curved glass and impressive brass hardware. On each side of the revolving door were redwood French doors. Inside the entrance on the left was a grand staircase to the second floor, a dormitory, where thirty-one rooms were rented to single men.

The first floor had a large reception desk where young swimmers lined up before 1:00 p.m., waiting for Mr. Moses to open the door leading to the pool. Once the door was opened, and Mr. Moses was sure the young swimmers had a pass, they ran down the hallway to the swimming pools as fast as they could. The air was filled with what, for Crockett children, were the scents of summer–chlorine and coconut-scented tanning cream. Mr. Moses could be heard yelling to stop running, but the children hurried, hoping to stake out a favorite spot on the wooden bleachers lining the pool. The most desirable spot was in the shade so as not to bake in the hot summer sun all afternoon.

But bake the young swimmers did, making it hard to walk home, tired, hungry, and sunburnt at the end of the day. Hungry swimmers bought Hershey's milk chocolate bars at the reception desk, eating them during rest periods when all the children had to vacate the pools for fifteen minutes. If the candy bars had melted in the sun, children eagerly used their fingers to scoop the chocolate into their anxiously awaiting mouths while others licked it off the slick white paper that wrapped the chocolate bar.

The lounge and reading room were furnished with Mission-style oak furniture and Victorian wicker. There was a card room and a gym with bleachers, which was said to be the first built in Contra Costa County. The gym had a distinctive aroma that emanated from its dark, stained redwood walls, wooden floor, tennis shoes, and sweat. Athletic

*The Crockett Club's main entrance
hall near the Reception Desk*

shoes, called tennis shoes at the time, could be heard
squeaking on the polished oak hardwood floors during all
sorts of matches or games, from badminton to basketball.

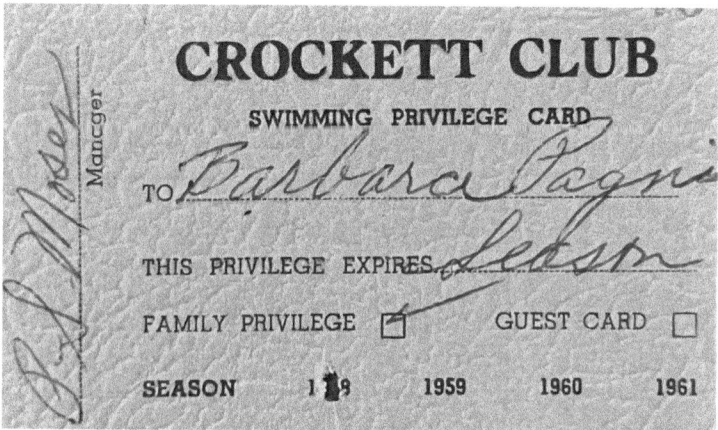

1958 Crockett Club Swim Pass

Every year in late spring, Crockett's children pestered their parents until they purchased summer swimming passes from Mr. Moses. The children didn't want to miss the fun, even one day of swimming with their friends. Two swimming pools accommodated swim classes and competitive swim teams. There was a shallow baby pool for those just learning to swim and a large pool, the big pool, for those who could. To gain swimming privileges in the big pool, young swimmers had to pass a test by swimming the width of the pool unaided. The swim trials were held every Friday.

The girls' dressing room was painted battleship grey and lit by a few low-level single incandescent light bulbs, rendering the dressing room dark, dank, and musty. There were individual dressing rooms where girls changed and left their clothes. It wasn't unusual to have one's underpants stolen as a prank, resulting in having to walk home commando sans panties. Wooden grates were installed over wet

The pool on a typical Crockett summer afternoon

concrete floors to prevent slips and falls. It was fun to step on the squishy foam mats by the showers that were soaked with a disinfectant meant to kill the fungus that caused athlete's foot.

The Crockett Club offered something for just about everybody. On the first level was a handball court and a billiards hall, and the basement housed a rifle range and a bowling alley. Wooden ballet barres lined the walls for ballet lessons just off the registration desk. Several sports teams were sponsored, including tennis, basketball, baseball, and softball for both men and women.

In addition, the club's large rooms held many dramatic and social events, including community dances, smokers, wrestling and boxing exhibitions, card parties, motion pictures, and swim meets. The Crockett Club was a splendid example of a thriving, extensively used community center.

Designed by architect William Crim of San Francisco, construction of the Community Auditorium followed. The impressive rock fireplace and fountain, which still exist today, were designed and built by Mr. Macchi, a gifted C&H Sugar gardener, stone mason, and an Italian immigrant. The Community Auditorium was dedicated on February 25, 1920, by Wallace Alexander, who had assumed the role of President of C&H Sugar when George Morrison Rolph became Chairman of the Board. President Alexander announced that the auditorium was a gift to all of Crockett's people. Concerned that residents would become dependent on the refinery and not feel a sense of civic responsibility, President Alexander noted that he hoped the hall would give each citizen an appreciation of his civic duty and would consent to donate a portion of their time and resources to community affairs. Perhaps this was the birth of Crockett's strong volunteer spirit, which is still vital and active today.

The Crockett Community Auditorium

Several distinguished guests, including the Archbishop of San Francisco, participated in the Auditorium's dedication, a celebration that drew 600 to 700 people. Most significant of these guests was James Rolph, Jr., George Morrison Rolph's older brother, then the mayor of San Francisco. James Rolph spoke eloquently of his brother, George, C&H Sugar's first Plant Manager, saying that George's heart was in Crockett. He added that George cared for nothing more than Crockett's residents, C&H Sugar employees, and their families. Once a company director, James noted that he had resigned from the Board during one of his mayoral campaigns.

James Rolph was so enthusiastic about Crockett's new Community Auditorium that he hoped to hold the next Republican National Convention in Crockett. President Alexander called George Morrison Rolph to the podium at the end of the speeches. Mr. Rolph said the auditorium was built for Crockett's families, children, and future. He continually considered C&H Sugar's workforce, legacy, and future planning. At the end of his speech, the audience sang, "For He's a Jolly Good Fellow!"

George Morrison Rolph's philosophy aligned with his brother James Rolph's progressive political style. It is easy to surmise that the two Rolph brothers influenced each others' thoughts. Known as Sunny Jim, James Rolph was the epitome of an optimistic, friendly, publicity-loving politician. Both brothers were skillful in getting things done and were adept in public relations. James Rolph was the Mayor of San Francisco for an unprecedented five terms and was known as the mayor of all people. His support was bi-partisan during his tenure. Gregarious and deeply committed to democratic values, in 1911, James received endorsements from both political parties, something unheard of today. Like his brother George, he considered himself an equal to those he encountered and governed. Known as a politician who practiced personality politics, James sought advice from experts in making important decisions. He was a progressive mayor who could boast many accomplishments, including the successful Panama Pacific International Exposition in 1915 and the erection of the Civic Center building after the devastating 1906 earthquake. In addition, he made significant steps towards ensuring an adequate San Francisco water supply and the development of the Municipal Railway.

James Rolph ended his political career as a Depression-era governor of California from 1931 to 1934. As Governor, his accomplishments included beginning work on the Colorado River Aqueduct and Boulder Dam. In 1932, he opened the Los Angeles Olympic Games. During his brief tenure, the California legislature ratified the Twenty-first Amendment to the U.S. Constitution, repealing prohibition. Rolph's administration also began planning for the Death Valley

National Monument. However, all was not sunny for Governor Rolph. He was criticized for approving legislation raising taxes on the poor and endorsed a brutal lynching in San Jose. In addition, some said he openly drank and ignored prohibition laws before the Twenty-first Amendment repealed prohibition.

George Morrison Rolph suffered a stroke on July 21, 1932, at age fifty-nine, at a Bohemian Club retreat at the Grove. He died within days at Stanford Hospital with his brother James, the Governor, by his side. On June 2, 1934, Governor James Rolph died while in office. On September 7, 1934, a resolution was passed by the California Toll Bridge Authority, dedicating the San Francisco-Oakland Bay Bridge to Governor Rolph in his memory.

Rolph Memorial Park with its fish ponds and bridges

So beloved was George Morrison Rolph in Crockett that in the fall of 1935, Rolph Memorial Park was dedicated to

Rolph's memory as a park and retreat. *The Honolulu Advertiser* noted that C&H Sugar donated the land. Local clubs, such as the Virtus Club and the Carquinez Women's Club, sponsored the park's planning and planting with the help of refinery engineers, architects, and landscaping experts as a lasting memory of George Morrison Rolph. The park became a natural retreat where wildflowers and shrubs native to California surrounded visitors.

Lilian Ashton Rolph donated an impressively designed stained glass window to St. Mark's Episcopal Church in memory of her late husband. The window, installed behind the altar, is constructed of antique fifteenth and sixteenth-century glass collected by the Rolphs on their European vacations.

On July 23, 1936, C&H Sugar published the first issue of its newsletter, *C&H News*. This was a precursor to *The Cubelet Press*, a community newsletter that lasted fifty-six years until 1992. When the first issue was published, the company employed an astounding 2,100 people at the refinery. At the time, Frank E. Sullivan, C&H Sugar's President, was concerned that with such a large workforce, people would lose touch. President Sullivan wrote an article about the importance of communicating the refinery owners' aims and objectives to support employees and emphasized the corporate board's need for all workers to be productive and efficient. He said the "chain is only as strong as its weakest link." President Sullivan wished to maintain the "friendly and cooperative spirit" between the company and its workers. This relationship had already existed for thirty years. President Sullivan believed that educating the company's workforce on the world of sugar and the political environment in which the industry operated was fundamental to maintaining this spirit. Fearing being misquoted, he wanted employees to hear news regarding their welfare candidly and honestly.

～

President Sullivan wrote, "Our lives, homes, families, and destinies are so closely linked with the welfare of C&H, particularly the Crockett refinery, that it is fitting and appropriate that this paper be issued." This statement is an excellent example of *Benessere* and expresses Crockett's Golden Age.

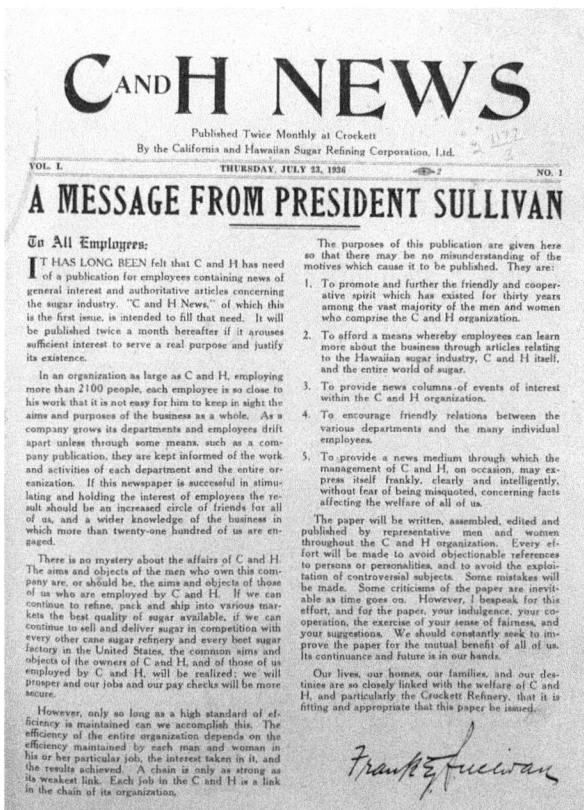

C<small>AND</small>H NEWS

Published Twice Monthly at Crockett
By the California and Hawaiian Sugar Refining Corporation, Ltd.

VOL. I.   THURSDAY, JULY 23, 1936   NO. 1

A MESSAGE FROM PRESIDENT SULLIVAN

To All Employees:

IT HAS LONG BEEN felt that C and H has need of a publication for employees containing news of general interest and authoritative articles concerning the sugar industry. "C and H News," of which this is the first issue, is intended to fill that need. It will be published twice a month hereafter if it arouses sufficient interest to serve a real purpose and justify its existence.

In an organization as large as C and H, employing more than 2100 people, each employee is so close to his work that it is not easy for him to keep in sight the aims and purposes of the business as a whole. As a company grows its departments and employees drift apart unless through some means, such as a company publication, they are kept informed of the work and activities of each department and the entire organization. If this newspaper is successful in stimulating and holding the interest of employees the result should be an increased circle of friends for all of us, and a wider knowledge of the business in which more than twenty-one hundred of us are engaged.

There is no mystery about the affairs of C and H. The aims and objects of the men who own this company are, or should be, the aims and objects of those of us who are employed by C and H. If we can continue to refine, pack and ship into various markets the best quality of sugar available, if we can continue to sell and deliver sugar in competition with every other cane sugar refinery and every beet sugar factory in the United States, the common aims and objects of the owners of C and H, and of those of us employed by C and H, will be realized; we will prosper and our jobs and our pay checks will be more secure.

However, only so long as a high standard of efficiency is maintained can we accomplish this. The efficiency of the entire organization depends on the efficiency maintained by each man and woman in his or her particular job, the interest taken in it, and the results achieved. A chain is only as strong as its weakest link. Each job in the C and H is a link in the chain of its organization.

The purposes of this publication are given here so that there may be no misunderstanding of the motives which cause it to be published. They are:

1. To promote and further the friendly and cooperative spirit which has existed for thirty years among the vast majority of the men and women who comprise the C and H organization.

2. To afford a means whereby employees can learn more about the business through articles relating to the Hawaiian sugar industry, C and H itself, and the entire world of sugar.

3. To provide news columns of events of interest within the C and H organization.

4. To encourage friendly relations between the various departments and the many individual employees.

5. To provide a news medium through which the management of C and H, on occasion, may express itself frankly, clearly and intelligently, without fear of being misquoted, concerning facts affecting the welfare of all of us.

The paper will be written, assembled, edited and published by representative men and women throughout the C and H organization. Every effort will be made to avoid objectionable references to persons or personalities, and to avoid the exploitation of controversial subjects. Some mistakes will be made. Some criticisms of the paper are inevitable as time goes on. However, I bespeak for this effort, and for the paper, your indulgence, your cooperation, the exercise of your sense of fairness, and your suggestions. We should constantly seek to improve the paper for the mutual benefit of all of us. Its continuance and future is in our hands.

Our lives, our homes, our families, and our destinies are so closely linked with the welfare of C and H, and particularly the Crockett Refinery, that it is fitting and appropriate that this paper be issued.

Frank E. Sullivan

*First edition of the C&H News,
the precursor to the Cubelet Press*

Chapter Three

Italian Immigrants Arrive

Just seven years into his tenure as refinery manager, and with a consistent supply of raw sugar cane arriving from the Hawaiian Islands, George Morrison Rolph still struggled to create a stable, productive workforce. Labor shortages endured. This critical challenge to C&H Sugar's productivity and growth can't be overstated. Mr. Rolph had to quickly implement a strategy to find and house employees to avoid the refinery closing as the Starr Flour Mill had done in the late 1800s. To mitigate this risk, the company opened its doors to immigrants. By 1923, 24 percent of C&H Sugar's production and warehouse employees were Italian immigrants, 7 percent were from Portugal, and 6 percent from Mexico. About 8 percent had emigrated from Great Britain. 12 percent of the total number of employees at the refinery were women. By 1928, the company employed 1,519 people, growing to over 2,000 employees before World War II. At its peak, 95 percent of the company's employees lived in Crockett.

How did Italian immigrants come to make up such a stunning percentage of C&H Sugar's workforce? Immigrants were eager to work to create a better life for their families. News of abundant work opportunities in California, specifically at the refinery, traveled locally by word of mouth and to Italy via letters sent home from family and friends already working at the factory. At that time, trans-Atlantic letters took months to arrive at their destinations because they were transported by sea. The ships that carried immigrants to and from the United States also transported letters and packages. Mail delivery by air did not exist. The first trans-Atlantic flight between the United States and Europe didn't occur until 1927 when Charles Lindbergh completed his solo flight coincidentally the same day the old Carquinez Bridge was dedicated.

By examining the stories of two Italian immigrant families who made their home in Crockett, why they decided to relocate, and what they left behind, one can better understand the shared experiences of so many immigrants living in Crockett. In the early 1900s, Carlo Magnaghi, a nineteen-year-old, strong, well-built, muscular young man with red hair, blue eyes, and a substantial bar-handled mustache, lived in Sant' Antonino Ticino, a neighborhood of Lonate Pozzolo, then a small village near Milan in Northern Italy. Like most young men, he dreamed of marrying his fiancé, Virginia Fassi, and starting a family. Discouraged because he couldn't find work in Italy, he lost hope for his future.

Virginia Fassi Magnaghi in 1913

Carlo received a letter from his cousin, Ambrogio Crivelli, who had emigrated to the United States some months before. The letter spoke of plentiful jobs in California, and Ambrogio invited Carlo to join him. Intrigued and trepid, Carlo boarded the ship "La Touraine," departing from Le Havre, France, a seaport city in northwest France 134 miles from Paris. He arrived at Ellis Island in New York on April 9, 1905, leaving behind his beloved fiancé, Virginia. Their separation would last five years.

The young immigrant spoke no English and traveled by rail across the United States. He arrived in San Francisco and settled in a rooming house in South San Francisco. Strong as an ox, Carlo found work as a stevedore on the San Francisco waterfront. One of his favorite stories recounted experiencing the San Francisco earthquake and fire a year later, on April 18, 1906, at 5:12 a.m. He spoke of his *padrona di casa,* 'landlady,' who was busy cooking breakfast at her massive cast iron wood stove, which was about five feet tall. The powerful tremor lasted less than a minute but was strong enough to cause the stove to fall forward just as his landlady stepped away. Carlo soon found himself providing voluntary labor to bury the earthquake and fire victims.

Leaving San Francisco, Carlo moved to Crockett and found steady employment at the refinery. He settled in a Valona boarding house near his extended family. His future life in Crockett was secure. Like most immigrants in Crockett, without knowing about or subscribing to the notion of the fabled American dream, Carlo found himself in the midst of it.

In 1909, Carlo returned to Italy to arrange Virginia's emigration to America. Once accomplished, he returned to the United States, leaving Virginia behind. Carlo landed on Ellis

Island on January 9, 1910, having seen the Statue of Liberty twice in his youth. He carried $40 in his pocket, equivalent to $1364 in 2024. Carlo's fiancé, Virginia Fassi, arrived at Ellis Island three years later on July 20, 1913. Imagine the sacrifice, the courage, and the fear this shy, quiet young woman must have experienced at leaving her small village at the age of twenty-two. She left her home, parents, sisters, and everything she had ever known and never returned. Virginia didn't speak English, yet with courage and grace, she boarded a ship in Le Havre and sailed alone to New York for four long weeks. Like Carlo, she too saw the Statue of Liberty, the vision of her future. Once Virginia had passed through customs, immigration officials guided her to a ferry that would take her to the train station. At that time, immigration authorities were careful to keep immigrants separate from the general population. Virginia boarded a train and rode cross-country, arriving at the Crockett Southern Pacific train depot on July 19, 1913. Today, that train station is the Crockett Historical Museum. Virginia put her complete faith and trust in Carlo, her fiancé, and married him on July 30, 1913, at St. Rose of Lima Catholic Church in Crockett. In subsequent years, three generations of their family would be married at St. Rose.

Just seven years after he arrived in America, on November 25, 1912, with fair wages from his job at C&H Sugar and a loan from his cousin Ambrogio, Carlo purchased two lots on Fifth Avenue in Valona and built two houses. This ability to buy property empowered Carlo and his family to enjoy economic stability and create comfortable savings. Creating modest wealth and passing it on to successive generations was the Italian immigrant way and the foundation for Carlo's family's upward economic mobility into America's lower middle class.

When Carlo's last surviving daughter, Louise, died in 2013 at the age of ninety-three, the deed to the family home revealed that Carlo had purchased his property on Fifth Avenue from John Muir, the famous writer and eccentric conservationist.

Muir deed for the Magnaghi family property at 1024 Fifth Avenue, Crockett

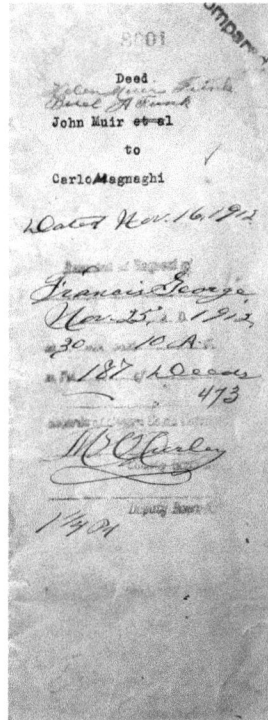

The purchase price was a shiny ten-dollar gold coin, as stated in the deed. Carlo built three living units—two flats in the large Victorian main house and a small bungalow with a basement on the back lot. Family members lived here for one hundred years, from 1913 to 2013. From 1939 to 1950, Carlo and his wife Virginia, their three daughters, spouses, and their children, a total of eleven people lived here as if

The Magnaghi family home on 5th Avenue in Valona

on a family compound. After World War II, in the early 1950s, Carlo's two daughters, Mary and Clementina, moved from Fifth Avenue to their own homes. Mary and her family moved to Lillian Street, and Clementina and her family moved to Seventh Avenue. Carlo's two sons-in-law, Ralph and Faustino, built their new houses. Louise, who never married, remained with her parents until they died in the early 1960s. Louise then lived alone until she died in 2012.

As they would have done in Italy, everyone pitched in with the cooking, childcare, and working in the vegetable garden. They fed the chickens and cleaned their coop when not working at the refinery. Those at home had to be quiet and mindful of those who slept during the day. Those who slept worked the "graveyard" shift at the refinery from 12:00 a.m. to 8:00 a.m. The refinery operated around the clock, 24/7, for "ten days on and four days off," as it was commonly described. The four days off were called shutdown,

**1969 C and H Sugar
Crockett Operating Calendar**

1969 C&H Sugar's Crockett Operating Calendar

when the plant was cleaned, maintained, and readied for the next ten days of production. Every refinery employee carried a small calendar the size of a business card to keep in their wallet. Significant family events couldn't be planned without consulting the shutdown calendar.

John Muir eventually owned property in Crockett when, at the age of forty-two, he married Louisa Wanda Strentzel, daughter of Dr. John Theophil Strentzel. Wanda Street in Crockett is named in Louisa's honor. The Muirs lived about ten miles east of Crockett in the Alhambra Valley in Martinez, California, where they raised their two daughters. Muir managed the family fruit ranch with his father-in-law, traveled, wrote, and advocated for wilderness preservation. He was famous for helping persuade President Theodore Roosevelt, Jr., the twenty-sixth United States President, to

John Muir and his family circa 1900 at the Muir home in Martinez, California. From left to right are daughters Wanda and Helen, Mrs. Muir and John Muir

establish Yosemite National Park. When Dr. Strentzel died on October 31, 1890, his Crockett property passed to his eldest daughter, Louisa Wanda Muir, his only remaining child. John Muir inherited the property when Louisa died in 1905.

Dr. Strentzel, who owned fifteen acres in Crockett's Valona neighborhood, a portion of the original Rancho Canada del Hambre land grant, was a Polish immigrant and political exile. In 1840, after fighting in the Polish Revolution in 1830, he fled to the United States to avoid being drafted into the Russian army. Dr. Strentzel settled first in Texas. After marrying Louisiana Erwin in 1849, he and Louisiana traveled to California. They made their first home along the Central Valley's Tuolumne River. Because of Louisiana's poor health and her need for a colder climate, the couple moved to Benicia and then to Martinez, settling in the Alhambra Valley. Dr. Strentzel built a family home that later became the home of John Muir.

Dr. John Theophil Strentzel

Dr. Strentzel came from a wealthy family, which enabled him to purchase twenty acres in the Alhambra Valley and achieve his dream of developing a horticultural business. Dr. Strentzel was a visionary, innovator, and entrepreneur. His pioneering agricultural methods yielded high-quality produce that commanded high prices in the San Francisco market. Most pertinent to this story, he was the city planner for Valona on Crockett's western slopes.

Dr. Strentzel named his community Valona for a European village he had visited. This village is likely the city of Vlore, Albania, whose name in Italian is *Valona*. Vlore is located on the Strait of Otranto, where the Adriatic meets the Ionian Sea, east of the heel of Italy's boot. Like Valona,

California, Vlore had a Mediterranean climate, including hot, dry summers and cool, wet winters.

After 1870, Valona developed organically into a small unincorporated village, following no rigid plan, on Crockett's bluffs. It wasn't much more than a neighborhood, settlement, hamlet, or whistle-stop with only several hundred houses clustered together. People with common interests, history, ethnicity, and socioeconomic status began to settle here, creating their permanent home base. What was the most common attribute its inhabitants shared? Immigration.

Immigrants from Southern Europe, Mediterranean countries including Portugal, Spain, and France, the American Dust Bowl, and Mexico settled here, with Valona's most significant population coming from Italy. There were so many immigrants in Valona that an assessment of C&H Sugar, written by Boris Emmit, Ph.D. from the Graduate School of Business and published in 1928 by Stanford University Press, referred to Valona as "the foreign element." Due to Italy's weak economy, three million Italians emigrated to the United States following World War I. Italians wanted to escape *miseria*, 'poverty,' unemployment, and hunger at home and sought new economic opportunities in America.

The wave of Italian immigrants to the United States at the end of the 19th and the beginning of the twentieth century was known as the "New Immigration" or "Second Wave." It consisted of immigrants from Europe, including Slavs and Jews as well. The previous period, or "Old Immigration," occurred throughout the nineteenth century and consisted primarily of immigrants from Scandinavia, Ireland, Germany, and Great Britain. Immigrants from the Old Immigration settled in Crockett on the more developed east side of town, east of Second Avenue. By contrast, immigrants from the "New Immigration" settled primarily on the west side in Valona, where land for building homes was plentiful and inexpensive.

Another Italian immigrant story is that of Alessandro Pagni. Alessandro was born in Florence and lived in Capannori, a small village near Lucca in Northern Italy. He had learned about Crockett and the refinery from his brother-in-law, Angelo Fanucchi, who had emigrated to Crockett in 1906. Alessandro arrived in Crockett in 1921, leaving his wife, Giuseppina, and three young boys, Rafaello, Faustino, and Medoro, behind in Capannori. Medoro was just a one-year-old infant. Alessandro was a *ritornati*, 'those that returned.' *Ritornati* planned to work, save wages, send money home to Italy to support their families, and eventually return. Alessandro and Giuseppina planned to buy land near their family in Capannori. For eight years, he worked at C&H Sugar without seeing his family. He lived in a boarding house in Valona and dutifully sent money home to Giuseppina. With these saved wages from C&H Sugar, Giuseppina fulfilled their dream by purchasing a small plot of land near her sister, Giuletta, in Capannori.

But the Pagni family's dream to live near their family in Italy proved short-lived. When Alessandro returned to Tuscany in 1929 expecting to remain, he was horrified to learn of threats to his family from Mussolini's Fascist Party. In the dead of night, four members of the local Fascist Party had banged on the family's front door, threatening his father-in-law, Fausto Guidi, who was in his mid-eighties. The Fascists were there to extort money from Fausto, pressuring him to join the Fascist Party. Responding to the loud pounding, Fausto opened a window on the second floor. After hearing the Fascist's demands, Fausto scurried from bedroom to

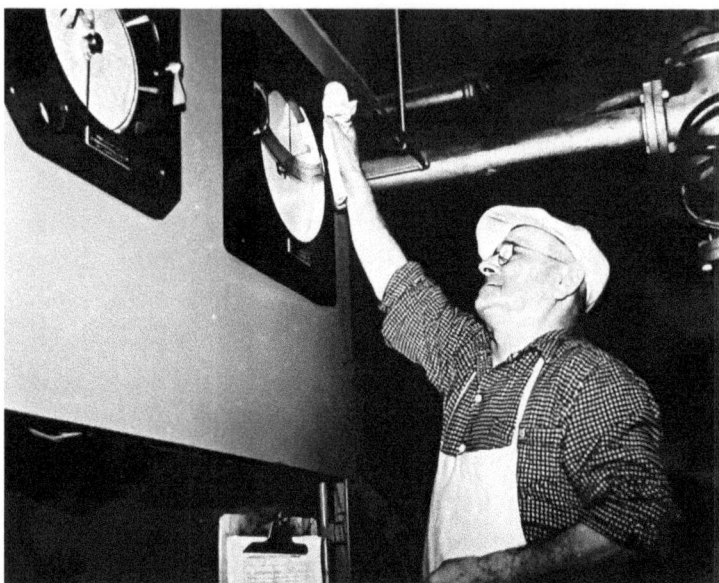

*Alessandro Pagni worked on the sanitation crew at
the refinery, always wearing his customary white hat*

bedroom with his grandson, Faustino, in tow, emptying
chamber pots into a bucket. Out the window went the foul
contents, dousing the Fascists who scurried off in the dark,
screaming like rats. During the night, the Fascists returned
and retaliated by quietly smearing human excrement on the
front door. The Fascists never bothered Fausto again, but his
family paid a heavy price by not receiving badly needed
food distributed by the party.

Witnessing the rise of Fascism and the changes that had
come to Italy under Mussolini's rule, Alessandro returned
to Crockett in 1929. He again left his family behind in Italy
until he could arrange their emigration. A job was waiting
for Alessandro at C&H Sugar when he returned. However, emigrating the whole family would prove to be a
daunting task.

Fausto and Luisa Lucchese Guidi. Fausto never gave in to Fascist extortion attempts and refused to join the Fascist Party.

In the early 1930s, the United States Congress decided too many Italians were living in the United States. To diminish these numbers, Congress passed more stringent laws, making immigration more difficult. Additionally, it was not unusual for some bureaucrats and government officials in Italy to make it difficult for those trying to emigrate to America. For example, to pass her physical exam, Alessandro's wife, Giuseppina, bribed an examining doctor to overlook the slight limp she had had since childhood. Her son, Faustino, although perfectly healthy, was required to have his tonsils removed. On the day of his tonsillectomy, Faustino walked to Lucca, about three kilometers away, just under two miles. After the procedure, he walked home, having had his tonsils removed without anesthesia.

In Valona, Alessandro asked Ben Zuppan, the proprietor

of a general store on Second Avenue, who had helped many immigrants, to help him navigate the complex immigration process. Mr. Zuppan helped Alessandro with language translations and gave him support, confidence, and encouragement. Mr. Zuppan's sponsorship assured United States immigration authorities that Alessandro was steadily employed and his family had a place to live.

The intersection of Pomona and Second Avenues. The Zuppan Bros. store is on the left.

The Pagni family's arrival in Crockett was staggered over two years. Alessandro returned in 1929. Ralph, his eldest son, arrived in 1930. Giuseppina arrived in Crockett with her two younger boys, Faustino and Medoro, on February 14, 1931. Departing on the SS Roma, like Virginia Fassi, they traveled in steerage, the lowest class of travel at the cheapest rate. Located in the ship's cargo hold, steerage was situated in the ship's bowels. It was crowded, dark, and damp, with limited sanitation facilities and no showers. Beds were

positioned along long rows, with some passengers sleeping
in shared bunks. No bed linens were provided, and mat-
tresses were commonly made of straw. The only fresh air
available came through the ship's small portholes, routinely
locked shut in rough seas. Not enough air and poor sanitary
conditions made the stench almost unbearable. Food provided by the shipping lines was often lukewarm soups,
black bread, boiled potatoes, or stringy beef, which had
likely been used to make stock for the first and second-class
passengers. Like cattle, hundreds of people were housed together, with little privacy or security.

*Pagni family ticket
from Genoa to New
York on board the
ship Roma*

Because of his extraordinary appetite, curiosity, and
sense of adventure, Faustino, at age fourteen, escaped the
dank steerage compartment daily to go up deck for his early
morning adventures. He returned to Giuseppina and
Medoro at night, armed with tall tales and food he had lifted

from the ship's upper levels stuffed in his pockets. Years later, at company events at the C&H Sugar's Guest Cottage, Faustino's friends from the refinery would check his sports coat pockets and laugh when they found leftovers hidden in a plastic bag. Little did they know this was a survival technique that had begun on his trans-Atlantic voyage to America. Faustino had a sense of adventure. He was curious, creative, confident, intelligent, and resourceful. While respectful, he challenged authority. Perhaps it was here on this passage that Faustino developed the attributes that would serve him well through war and hunger. He learned to be an observer and organizer and to plan an exit strategy when the situation dictated. Faustino taught his children that having the skills necessary to survive was paramount.

Pagni family passport

When Giuseppina arrived in New York, she and her two sons visited her brother, Elia Guidi, and his family. Most memorable for Faustino was encountering his cousins for the first time in New York. When the girls asked him to sharpen their pencils, he went to their basement to retrieve a carpenter's plane. The girls laughed, then showed him how to sharpen a pencil using a hand-cranked pencil sharpener. Faustino never forgot that lesson, as it was one of his first experiences of how his life in America would differ from that in Italy. He was provincial, from the country, and not used to such conveniences.

Encouraged and rested, Giuseppina and her boys boarded a train and began their trip across the country to Crockett. They had a short layover at Chicago's huge Union Train Station, the Midwest's vast flagship train station. Giuseppina decided to treat her boys to a chocolate bar, as she had often done when they visited Lucca. Encouraged to find an Italian vendor to help her, she eagerly handed over her last five-dollar bill. Her friendly countryman assured Giuseppina he would return with her change, but he never did. Suddenly, the trip across the country became a nightmare. However, Giuseppina was spunky and resourceful and visited the train's dining car nightly, begging for bread. A compassionate train steward sympathizing with Giuseppina ensured she and her boys had a piece of bread slathered with butter and sprinkled with salt every night from Chicago to San Francisco. Faustino never recovered from this experience of hunger for the rest of his life.

Arriving in Truckee and thinking she was finally in Crockett, Giuseppina began to disembark, but a kind, attentive train conductor stopped her. Finally arriving in Crockett in the dark six hours later, Giuseppina was relieved to have made this monumental journey on her own with her sons. Alessandro watched his family disembark from the train. His friend, Mr. Zuppan, stood at his side. Faustino never forgot the large headlights on Mr. Zuppan's car and how they illuminated the train station in the darkness. He had never seen anything like this before.

Imagine. The Pagni family's journey to Crockett began in Capannori with a ride to the train station in Lucca in a horse-drawn cart driven by Americo, a family friend. It ended with a ride to their new home in a modern automobile with impressively large headlights, driven by their new friend, Mr. Zuppan. The Pagni family's first home, rented from the Biagi family, was a small flat on Lillian Street. All three families–the Pagnis, Zuppans, and Biagis would remain lifelong friends. The apartment was on Lillian Street, a block from the Magnaghi family. In the ensuing years, two Pagni brothers, Ralph and Faustino, would marry two Magnaghi sisters, Mary and Clementina, a practice not uncommon in Valona.

~

Often gruff and stern, Giuseppina had a special place in her heart for those less fortunate than she. She was also a devout Roman Catholic and had a deep faith. She regularly sent money and clothing packages home to her family in Italy and helped those in her new community. Several transients, then called hobos, periodically rode the rails through Crockett and stopped at Giuseppina's house for food. She never let them enter the house, but they sat on the concrete stairs leading from her home to Del Mar Circle. She fed the men homemade minestrone soup, a staple in her refrigerator, with a slice of Alessandro's homemade Tuscan bread. Perhaps feeding these hungry strangers was Giuseppina's way of repaying the kindness shown to her on her cross-country journey to her new home, Crockett, in her new country.

Chapter Four
Creating an Italian Village in Valona

Life in the United States didn't suit everyone. Many Italian immigrants came with the idea of working to support their families in Italy and eventually repatriating. Immigrants worked hard. They paid for their living expenses in Crockett, sending the remainder of their paychecks to their families in Italy, never expecting to become United States citizens. Called *ritornati*, 'those that returned,' these workers numbered about 50 percent of Italian immigrants in the United States. In 1927, approximately 11 percent of C&H Sugar employees quit their jobs to return home. Employee turnover was a considerable challenge for the refinery because, by 1928, roughly 20 percent of the refinery's workforce of 1,519 were Italian immigrants.

Most Italians working at the refinery chose to live in Valona because almost everyone living there spoke standard Italian if not their region-specific dialect. Speaking English wasn't required to work at the refinery as many workers and supervisors were fluent in Italian.

Carlo Magnaghi worked as a stevedore on the C&H Sugar docks, unloading one-hundred-twenty-five-pound raw sugar sacks from the cargo holds of ships from Hawaii. Working in pairs, each man grabbed one end of a heavy hemp or burlap sack and threw it onto a cart to be wheeled into the refinery. Carlo continued at this job until he injured his back. He was then transferred to the sanitation department, where he worked as a janitor with Alessandro Pagni, whose two sons, Rafaello and Faustino, would one day marry Carlo's two daughters, Mary and Clementina.

To support, educate, and guide non-English speakers on their path to citizenship, the company sponsored "Americanization" classes at John Swett High School. Classes were

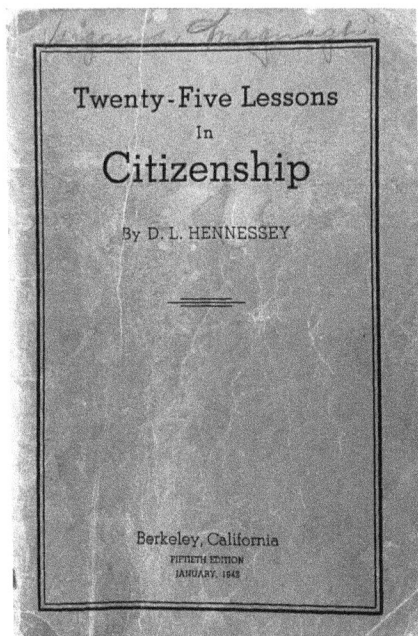

Twenty-Five Lessons
In
Citizenship

By D. L. HENNESSEY

Berkeley, California
FIFTIETH EDITION
JANUARY, 1943

The book Virginia Fassi used to study for her citizenship test was written in English

taught by trained supervisors from the refinery. The courses included instruction in English and citizenship and taught immigrants what it meant to be an American. The company also created an English textbook with common phrases used in the refinery. It was common for some family members to be naturalized citizens while others were not. This would prove consequential for many Crockett families after World War II's outbreak.

In 1940, Congress passed the Alien Registration Act,

which made it illegal for anyone living in the United States to advocate for the violent overthrow of the government. The act required all non-citizens to register with the government between August 27 and December 26, 1940. The purpose of this registration was to identify the location of

Form AR-1

UNITED STATES DEPARTMENT OF JUSTICE
IMMIGRATION AND NATURALIZATION SERVICE
ALIEN REGISTRATION DIVISION
WASHINGTON, D. C.

THE NATIONAL REGISTRATION OF ALIENS

INSTRUCTIONS FOR REGISTRATION AND SPECIMEN FORM

To Every Alien in the United States:

A Nation-wide registration of aliens will be conducted from August 27 to December 26, 1940.

All aliens 14 years of age or older are required to register. Alien children under 14 years must be registered by their parents or guardians. Generally speaking, foreign-born persons who have not become citizens of the United States are aliens. Persons with first citizenship papers must register.

To make your registration easier, you should fill out pages 3 and 4 of this form and personally take it to the post office. *This is not the actual registration form,* but it shows the information that you must give at the post office when you register. There you will be asked to give the information indicated on these pages, to swear to (or affirm) its truth, and to be fingerprinted.

The registration of aliens is compulsory. A specific act of Congress—the Alien Registration Act of 1940—requires all aliens to register during the official registration period, August 27 to December 26, 1940. All aliens 14 years of age or over must be fingerprinted as a part of registration. A fine of $1,000 and imprisonment for 6 months is prescribed by this law for failure to register, for refusal to be fingerprinted, or for making registration statements known to be false.

Registration is free. You should not pay anyone to register for you. It is not necessary to pay any person or group to assist you in registering. The Government, through its post offices, will assist you as much as possible. Complete instructions and the official regulations for registration may be examined at registration post offices.

The Alien Registration Act was passed so that the United States could determine exactly how many aliens there are, who they are, and where they are Registration, including fingerprinting, will not be harmful to law-abiding aliens. All records will be kept secret and confidential and will be made available only to such persons as may be designated with the approval of the Attorney General of the United States.

Attention of all citizens as well as aliens is called to the laws of the United States which protect aliens in this country.

A receipt card will be sent to every alien who registers. This card will serve as evidence of registration.

After registration, the law requires all aliens and parents or guardians of aliens to report changes of residence address within 5 days of the change to the Immigration and Naturalization Service, Department of Justice, Washington, D. C. You can get change of address forms at post offices.

All aliens in the United States are urged to comply fully with the provisions of the Alien Registration Act of 1940.

Fill out the enclosed sample form and bring it with you to the post office when you register. Do not delay your registration. Complete it as soon as possible.

Earl G Harrison

EARL G. HARRISON,
Director of Registration.

10—16201

The National Registration of Aliens form

non-citizens. Registration was *compulsory BUT free*. Like many of Crockett's non-citizens who couldn't read, write, or speak English, Virginia Magnaghi and Giuseppina Pagni, with their children's help, dutifully registered at the post office on Rolph Avenue. No one could have imagined what this would mean.

In March 1938, Hitler's armed forces began the Blitzkrieg, Lightning War. In contemporary terms, Hitler's strategy was to move fast, using shock and awe to catch countries off-guard and ill-prepared. At the beginning of the war, invaded countries didn't put up much of a fight, though a robust resistance movement developed in each country in the ensuing years. Storming their way across Europe, the Nazis occupied country after country. Czechoslovakia and Austria were the first to be occupied by Germany in March 1938. Poland was conquered in September 1939, followed by Denmark and Norway in February 1940. Hitler's stormtroopers bombed and invaded Belgium and the Netherlands in May of the same year. In June 1940, France and Britain's Channel Islands were invaded and occupied by German armed forces. Germany attacked the Soviet Union in June 1941 but was thwarted by the Russian winter. Germany then turned against its former ally and occupied Italy in October 1943. The Italian home of Giuseppina Pagni's sister, Giuletta, was occupied by two German officers. She lived in Capannori with her children while her husband was away fighting in North Africa with the Italian army. According to family lore, Giuletta, confident and formidable, warned the two officers that she would kill them if they touched her two daughters. The officers never did.

Europe's last independent country, Great Britain, was left to fight Hitler's forces. Its intrepid leader, Winston

Churchill, sought help from the United States, but the American people made it clear to President Roosevelt that they wanted to stay uninvolved and out of Europe's war. The United States struggled to maintain its neutrality. In early 1941, before Pearl Harbor, Faustino Pagni, now a United States citizen, wanted to see the world and enlisted in the United States Army with many of his local friends. When Japan bombed Pearl Harbor on December 7, 1941, the decision to enter the war was made for the United States, and everything changed for Crockett's citizens and enlisted men. Faustino Pagni was stationed at Fort Lewis, Washington, on that fateful day. He spoke about how the enlisted men at the Fort were quickly hidden in Washington forests, fearing that an attack on the base was imminent. President Roosevelt mobilized the country and its industries to fight the war in the South Pacific and Europe, and the people of the United States responded fervently.

By 1943, many Crockett men and women who hadn't volunteered for the war effort worked at the refinery as essential workers. Non-citizen immigrants living in Crockett and its Valona neighborhood were identified as enemy aliens, taken into custody, and interned by the government. Crockett was in a sensitive evacuation zone because of its proximity to the Mare Island Navel Shipyard in Vallejo and the Port Chicago Navel Weapons Station in Concord. Virginia Magnaghi and Giuseppina Pagni were interned with Giuseppina's youngest son, Pino. At the time, Pino was nine years old, and no one was at home to care for him since every other family member was working at the refinery. At the beginning of their internment, the three spent two weeks in Berkeley at a home on 10th Street. They were then transferred to St. Helena in Napa Valley. The United States government held them captive for three months until President Roosevelt declared that Italians were no longer a threat to the United States. In fact, Italians were needed for war production.

Today, we know quite a lot about the internment of Japanese-Americans and their struggles and losses. However, few still don't know what had happened to the Italians. Virginia and Giuseppina never talked about their detention. This sad chapter of Italian-American history, called *il nostro segreto,* 'our secret,' was *una vergogna,* 'a shame.' Shame in Italian culture is to be avoided at all costs. After their return to Valona, both women attended company-sponsored Americanization classes at the high school. On May 29, 1944, they became citizens. The program was held at the John Swett High School auditorium. With their citizenship certificates and tiny American flags in hand, they could finally put their internment nightmare behind them.

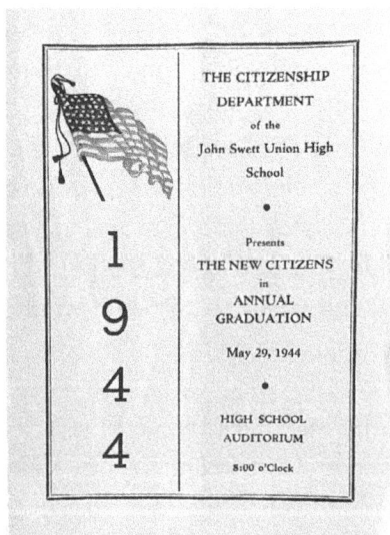

Program for the Annual Graduation of New Citizens, 1944

𝔓𝔯𝔬𝔤𝔯𝔞𝔪

Mrs. Ramona Ceceña Ward, *Presiding*

Vocal Solos · · · · · · · · · Miss Arabelle Hong
"Perhaps" · · · · · · · · · *de Segurola*
"Love Call" from "Rose Marie" · · · · · *Friml*
Accompanist, Mrs. Frances Lozier

"My Experiences as a Japanese Prisoner" · Miss Faye Kilpatrick
Teacher of English, Vacaville Union High School

Selections · · · · · · · · Instrumental Quartet
"Forosetta" — Tarantelle · · · · · · · *Arditi*
"Morris Dance" from "Henry VIII" · · · *German*
Melodie from "Orpheus" · · · · · · · *Gluck*
Overture to "The Merry Wives of Windsor" · · *Nicolai*
Mr. Bernard G. Marshall, Director, Clarinet;
Miss Harriet Marshall, Flute; Mrs. Sylvia Cugley, 'Cello;
Mrs. Frances Lozier, Piano

Presentation of Class · · · · · · Mr. Jefferson Cralle
Principal, John Swett Union High School

Awarding of Diplomas · · · · · Mr. Jack Merchant
Clerk, High School Board of Trustees

Greetings to the New Citizens · · · · · Mr. A. C. Dyer
Americanism Chairman, Crockett Post, American Legion

Presentation of Flags and Flag Codes · - Mrs. Mildred Nelson
Americanism Chairman, Crockett Post,
American Legion Auxiliary

Pledge to the Flag · · · · · American Legion Auxiliary
Crockett Unit

"Star-Spangled Banner" · · · · Miss Hong and Quartet

NEW CITIZENS OF 1943-44

Dorothy L. Lewis, *Director of Citizenship*

Ersilia Airoldi	Santina Marella
Maria Airoldi	Augusta Martin
Guiseppa Alfieri	Teresa Mossina
Internazionale Bortolussi	Maria Moutinho
Rosalia Bottarini	Louise Antonietta Noe
Joseph Bottero	Mary Oliveira
Maria Canetta	Josephine Pagni
Luigia Canziani	Maria Pallotta
José Cardoza	Elizabeth Paoli
Maria Da Re	John C. Pitta
Maria Faria	Teresa Quilici
Angelina Ferrini	Antonio Roque
Maria José Garcez	Arminda Sacco
Demetra Gravanis	Merced Sepulveda
Anna Marta Gregoris	Manuel Souza
Louise Lopez	Gregorio Travaglini
Virginia Magnaghi	Charles George Vergopulos
	Ramona Cerena Ward

Ushers — Sea Scouts of the Ship "Golden Hind"

Program interior documents the nationalization
of several Crockett and Valona families

Italian emigres in Valona wanted to live amongst neighbors who shared their cultural traditions, values, beliefs, customs, cuisine, language, religion, arts, music, and the importance of their children's education to succeed in their new country. Some of these cultural norms, which dated back to the late nineteenth century, hadn't changed or evolved in America as they had in Italy. Most immigrants were passionate about keeping their culture alive and were committed to passing their traditions to their children and future generations.

For example, it was an Italian tradition for a young girl to begin filling a hope chest with the hand-embroidered linens she would need for her future home. The chest, made of wood, was lined with fragrant cedar to conserve fine linens for a lifetime. Many young women bought their cedar hope chests at Toretta's Toggery on Flora Street and First Avenue in Valona, run by the Toretta brothers. Others bought their chests at the Crolona Furniture Store, run by Mr. Simontacchi, on Loring Avenue. The Crolona Furniture Store gave each Crockett young woman high school graduate a miniature promotional chest as a graduation gift, hoping they would purchase a cedar chest there.

Many girls started their hope chests at the young age of twelve. This required learning to sew and embroider. Mothers, grandmas, and aunts taught these fundamental skills just as they had been taught by their mothers, relatives, or friends. Carquinez Grammar School also taught gender-based skills to its students. While boys learned woodworking, the girls learned how to cook, sew, and manage a household. Many older women from Italy and Portugal practiced and taught their complex skills of *ricamo ad intaglio*, 'cutwork embroidery,' and shared their intricate patterns with each other. Most continued to make tablecloths

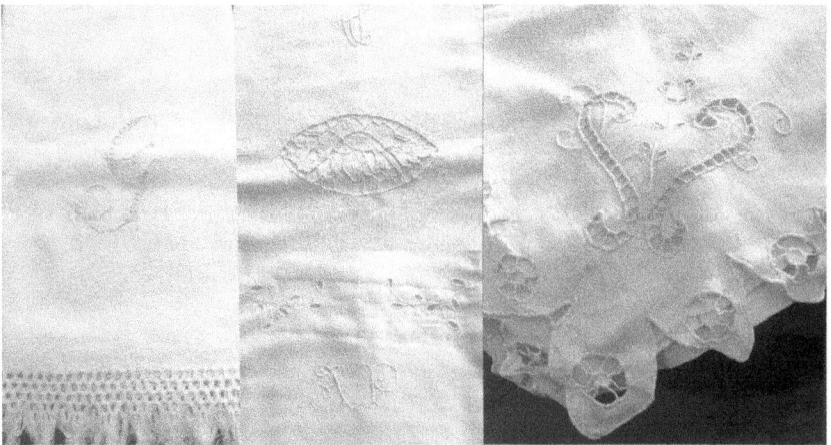

Italian cutwork embroidery, ricamo ad intaglio

and pillowcases until their eyes began to fail them in old age. Misprinted one-hundred-pound C&H Sugar sacks discarded by the refinery made their way to Crockett and Valona's homes. They were washed, bleached to remove the ink, and sewn into pillowcases, towels, and sheets.

Young girls usually started learning their skills by embroidering simple day-of-the-week kitchen towels ordered from Herrschner's, a mail-order catalog of stitchery and craft kits. The towels illustrated the chores a woman was expected to accomplish during the week: washing on Monday, ironing on Tuesday, mending and sewing on Wednesday, tending the vegetable garden on Thursday, cleaning the house on Friday, baking on Saturday, and relaxing on Sunday. The illustrations communicated what a girl's future held for her.

It was a challenge for first-generation children to balance parents' or grandparents' insistence on maintaining old country traditions while fitting in with their peers in modern California, the new country. This expectation often caused conflicts among generations, between immigrants and their children. Negotiations were commonplace, resulting in noisy arguments that could go on for days. In the end, compromises were reached, and everyone reconciled. Families lived near each other, and it was common for homes to be multi-generational or for families to live side-by-side. There wasn't much privacy. Grandparents saw their children and grandchildren several times every day, and it was common for grandmothers to lecture their *nipotini*, 'grandchildren,' in Italian. These sermons were often delivered *ad alta voce* 'in a loud voice,' in Italian, arms flailing to make a point. Grandchildren didn't always have the language skills necessary to respond because Italian wasn't always taught at home. Italian wasn't taught at home because foreign-speaking parents wanted their children to learn English so they would not draw attention to themselves. Family members had likely suffered discrimination and internment during World War II, and the parents wanted their children to assimilate quickly.

Nonnas, 'grandmothers,' usually wore an apron over their cotton dresses. It didn't matter that the two fabrics didn't match or coordinate. Nonnas could be found sitting at a

Giuseppina Pagni keeping watch over Seventh Avenue and Del Mar Circle in Valona

kitchen window or on the back porch as if serving as an army sentry. Perhaps they were the precursors to a neighborhood watch program. Nonnas surveyed the neighborhood from their perch while reading the Italian newspaper, petting their cat, crocheting a tablecloth, edging a kitchen towel, or drinking a cup of *camomilla*, 'chamomile tea.' Sometimes, they'd open a window and yell at a neighbor if something was not to their liking. As a child, getting away with bad behavior was hard as mothers often received telephone calls about their children's missteps before they reached home. It was common for Italian mothers to defend their children's behavior outside the home, but privately, they were stern disciplinarians.

Children growing up in Crockett and Valona in the mid-twentieth century were often oblivious to their advantages, living in what can be called Crockett's Golden Age that lasted from approximately the second decade of the 1900s through the mid-1970s. From the1800s to the 1960s, Crockett was self-sufficient and geographically isolated from the rest of the Bay Area. Crockett's approximately 5,000 residents were provided with everything they needed – employment, food, supplies, stores, services, entertainment, and jobs at the refinery within walking distance from home. Property and rents were inexpensive. Many housing types were

*Photo showing a geographically
isolated Crockett in the early 1920s*

available depending on a person's marital status, socioeconomic status, and immigration status. Many of Crockett's early immigrants built homes and boarding houses, providing much-needed housing for those who came later, and families made extra money by renting out rooms. Despite not speaking English, women like Virginia Magnaghi frequently offered meals, alterations, or laundry services to single working men.

For some immigrants, assimilation to life in America was complicated, often tricky, and sometimes made them sad or depressed. Carlo Magnaghi once commented, *"C'e' un aeroplano nella soffita che un giorno ci porterà tutti a casa,"* meaning, 'There is an airplane in the attic that will one day take us all home.' This simple sentence reflects the heartache Carlo and many immigrants felt. While working hard to build a new life in America, Carlo deeply mourned what he had left behind in Italy and daydreamed about going home. Others, by contrast, understood that their present and future were here in America. However, they fantasized about their early life in Italy, their home country. Stories of their early lives became *favole*, 'fairytales,' fantasies. When subsequent generations visited the family's hometown in Italy, they were often disappointed that the family village didn't live up to the expectations created by their parents' stories.

Italian immigrants in Crockett infused their love and zest for life into their new realities in Valona to ease such heartaches. Their memories, strong work ethic, skills, and abundant energy helped them recreate their view of an Italian village and community in the Bay Area. Homes rose in layers mimicking the contours of the steep hillsides that descended to the straits. They were surrounded by terraced *orti*, 'vegetable gardens, *frutteti*, 'orchards,' and *vigne*, 'vineyards.' Gardens were planted with the precious seeds immigrants brought from Italy, often concealed in their *baule*, 'large steamer trunks,' or their undergarments. For example, some of these seeds were for heirloom tomatoes and "*borlotti*" beans.

Alessandro Pagni and his friend and neighbor Amato Baccetti planted tomatoes from the heirloom seeds they brought from Italy. To ensure they could always grow their special heirloom tomatoes year after year, they used an age-old practice from Italy, saving and conserving seeds from their crop's biggest, tastiest tomatoes at the end of the season. They collected the seeds by cutting and wetting a small piece of cotton muslin cloth and squeezing the seeds from the tomato onto the fabric. The muslin was set in the sun to dry. Once dried, the muslin was rolled up, placed in a paper bag, and hung on a clothesline in a cool, dark, dry place in their basements for planting the following year. When Alessandro and Baccetti died, the practice was passed on to

Heirloom tomato seeds from Italy saved the old-fashioned way

Alessandro's sons, Ralph and Faustino. Every February until Faustino was well into his nineties, he sowed the heirloom tomato seeds he had saved from the previous year. In late spring, Faustino generously gave the tomato seedlings to his family and friends in the neighborhood.

Residents made cuttings of their favorite flowers and shared them with friends. It wasn't unusual for neighbors to take cuttings as they walked past a neighbor's house. Soon, the cuttings took root and flourished in their gardens. Lavender plants bloomed in almost every garden. Their flowers were used to make sachets and placed in drawers and closets to scent the contents and prevent pests like moths. Dried lavender flowers were thought essential to preserve cherished family handmade linens.

Gardens were a source of pride, and Valona's hillsides reflected those of Italy. For example, abalone shells, harvested from the Sonoma coast by avid local divers, were an essential garden accessory. Placing a shell at the base of a plant or tree to be irrigated, savvy gardeners lay the end of their hose inside the shells. Water was turned on slowly, at a drip, enabling the water to soak the soil through the natural holes in the shell. This method provided a drip irrigation method and prevented soil erosion.

It's possible today to travel to Italy and find many landscaping design details in Italian gardens similar to those in Valona. Materials were used, fences were designed, tomatoes were cultivated, and beans were staked in a manner still found in Italy. In Valona, almost everyone raised chickens for eggs and meat. Some residents raised rabbits, which they sold or traded with friends. In addition, rabbit manure was mixed with water to make a "tea" to fertilize certain plants, and chicken manure was worked into the soil. Compost piles were a must.

*Alessandro Pagni and his daughter-in-law Mary in
the orto (vegetable garden). The beans are staked just
as they would have been in Capannori, Italy*

Ralph Pagni was an expert mushroom forager, hunting
prized Porcini mushrooms that were eaten fresh or dry.
Ralph and his wife, Mary, carefully prepared the Porcini to
dry in their living room in the fall and early winter after the
first rain. Their wood fireplace provided warmth to dry the
Porcini placed on wooden screened frames on a bed of fresh
bay leaves Ralph foraged in the Valona hills. He had many
secret foraging spots in Napa Valley, and his favorite mushroom foraging spot for button mushrooms was in the sheep-
grazing fields of Vacaville. When Ralph died, his treasured
mushroom hunting locations died with him.

As in Italy, Valona gardens were planted and harvested
according to the lunar calendar. For example, vegetables

growing above the soil were seeded with a rising moon, while vegetables growing underground, such as beets and carrots, were sown with a waning moon. Italians ate local food according to the seasons. Many organic and bio-dynamic growing philosophies and techniques popular today were commonly used in Italy and Valona generations ago.

Nearly every house in Valona had a damp, chilly basement, perfect for storing preserved food and wine. There was a cabinet with screened doors for ventilation to hang, cure, and age prosciutto and salami. Shelves were laden with jars of *conserva*, 'homemade tomato sauce.' For convenience, almost everyone had a second kitchen in the basement. One could walk through the neighborhood in late summer and early fall and smell the aroma of tomatoes cooking on an old stove in a neighbor's basement. Many Italian women cooked *conserva* in the cool cellar because it was so hot outside. The basement doors and windows were open so the heat from the cooking could escape along with the aroma. The basement kitchen was also easier to clean because it had a cement floor.

Basements had ample space for a redwood tank for fermenting grapes and storing wine barrels and bottles. Clementina Magnaghi Pagni often mentioned that she hated late summer and fall in Valona because her father sent her and her sisters to his friends' houses to help crush grapes. Hearing a truck loaded with grapes laboring up steep Fifth Avenue, Clementina knew it was time for her and her sisters to dash off, wash their feet, and get into the tank and crush.

By contrast, many children loved this time of year because it meant the beginning of the grape harvest and crush. Great fun! Hearing a truck loaded with wooden lugs filled to the brim with grapes, still warm from the hot California

Indian summer sun, children dropped whatever they were doing. They ran as fast as they could to the crush, where the family happily gathered. The men shouted with gusto. The Pagni brothers joked, teased one another mercilessly, laughed like children, and drank wine from last year's vintage. One of the brothers, usually Faustino, would start singing an old folk song from Capannori. The sound of the gravity-driven crusher and its intermittent stops provided percussion. Fruit flies were everywhere. Local families applied for wine-producing permits issued by the U.S. Treasury Department Alcohol Tax Unit in San Francisco. Still in effect today in California, a permit was required to make 100 gallons of wine annually if only one adult lived in the household; 200 gallons could be produced if two or more adults lived together.

Carlo Magnaghi's permit from the United States Treasury Department to make 200 gallons of wine

Memories of Italian village life also played out at the brick warehouse on Lillian and Sixth Streets that once housed the Crockett Soda Works. Next to the warehouse was a tiny house called the *stanzing*, a 'small room.' Here, retired men gambled and played Italian card games, such as *Briscola* or Scopa. They also played *bocce ball* in the courts in the adjacent yard, just as they would have done in Italy.

The men of Valona gathered at the stanzing 'little room' to play cards and bocce ball in the adjacent lot by the Basetti family. Note the fedora hats.

The men wore long-sleeved shirts with "sleeve garters" above their elbows. At that time, men's shirts came in one standard sleeve length and had no buttons at the cuff. Sleeve garters made the sleeves the correct length, so the men didn't have to roll their sleeves or soil their cuffs. The sleeve garter caused the shirt sleeve to balloon above the elbow, making the sleeves resemble those found on vintage Victorian dresses.

The men wore fedora hats, and many smoked "*Toscanelli*" cigars, filling the room with a distinct acrid

Alessandro Pagni wearing sleeve garters, as was customary for the time

odor. Spittoons were scattered around the floor between the round tables, and the beer flowed freely. The men were visible through a smoke-filled haze, slapping their cards down on the table, dramatizing their move by yelling, "Tah!" as they did so. The men often addressed each other using *sopranomi,* 'nicknames,' a common tradition in Italy. Sometimes, *nonnos'* grandfathers' invited their grandchildren inside for a cool soda. A group of neighborhood children would often sit on the steps outside the *stanzing* and eavesdrop, enjoying all the laughter and loud conversations in Italian rising from this small space. Even though the children couldn't speak Italian, they understood it very well, unbeknownst to the adults. They often used this skill to their advantage.

When Valona residents died, some of their families shipped their remains to their villages in Italy to be buried there with their *parenti,* 'relatives.' Elderly widowed women in Valona dressed in black to honor their deceased husbands just as they would have in Italy. With their husbands gone, they continued to live near their children, working hard by helping to care for their grandchildren. They did laundry, ironed, grew fruit and vegetables in their gardens, and prepared traditional foods. On Halloween, mothers would ask their children to Trick-or-Treat at these widows' homes so the widows would have visitors during the day. Trick or Treaters were often disappointed when, instead of candy, the elderly women placed a few unshelled walnuts, a piece of fruit from their yard, or a few pennies in their bags. These treats were what they would have put in their children's shoes in Italy for the Feast of La Befana, celebrated at Advent after Christmas.

Knowing how to fish and properly handle a Daisy BB gun was popular while growing up in Valona. Children were adept at using slingshots and bows and arrows, storing multiple arrows in quivers slung over their shoulders their mothers had sewn. Some Italian immigrants in Crockett and Valona came from fishing villages in Sicily and developed an enduring relationship with the straits. When commercial fishing was allowed in the straits, a small fishing village grew along Crockett's shoreline east of the refinery. Dowrelio's Boat Works, a full-service boat works and deepwater harbor at the foot of Port Street offered an extensive wharf for anglers of all ages. It also provided boat berthing and several services for fishermen, including boat repair, a bait shop, and chartered fishing excursions.

Members of the Crockett Bass Club, organized in 1926, volunteered their spare time and labor to build wharves and buildings that are still used today. The Pagni brothers, members of the club, made more than one rowboat, which they regularly used for bass fishing. They had to climb down a

*A walk to Dowrelio's Marina was
always a treat and an adventure*

steep ladder secured with pullies and long ropes to reach
the boat from the club's wooden boardwalk. The distance
could be six to eight feet, depending on the tide. The water
was always choppy; surprisingly, no one fell in. Never own-
ing a motor, Faustino Pagni thought nothing of rowing his
children to the original bridge's center pier, braving the
choppy waters and strong currents without life jackets.
Faustino couldn't swim, and his children weren't strong
enough swimmers to handle the rough waters of the Carquinez Straits should an emergency arise. Foolishly, that

The Pagni brothers' rowboat at the Crockett Bass Club

didn't stop them. Faustino told the story of his friend Jim, who fished under the center pier amidst the old wooden pilings, a great place for bass to hide. Jim hadn't kept track of time or the tide and got caught under the pier. He lay in his rowboat, waiting hours for the ebbtide before he could escape his watery confinement. How dark and eerie that experience must have been.

Daisy BB guns could be purchased at Pedrotti Hardware on Second Avenue, and many Crockett parents did just that for their children. Opening a new cardboard cylinder full of shiny, polished copper bee bees was a special treat. Once the children had attended gun safety classes at the Crockett Club, parents trusted their children to handle their guns safely. However, sometimes, the children got into mischief, often shooting each other. Parents were never told. Alessandro Pagni hired his grandchildren to hunt robins, paying twenty-five cents per bird, to make his famous Tuscan bird stew, which he served over polenta. The robins tasted gamey, and their legs were so tiny they didn't seem worth eating. For Alessandro, an extraordinary traditional Tuscan cook, robin stew reminded him of home.

Italian cultural values dictated a hierarchical loyalty first to the family, then to neighbors and close friends. Principles such as these provided the foundation for shared friendships and bonds between the residents of Crockett, its Valona neighborhood, and, most notably, the women working at the refinery. Since many lived in Valona, these Italian families shared all their lives—in work and play, from birth to death.

Because most families owned only one car and mothers generally didn't drive, Valona's children walked to and from school and extracurricular activities such as sports practices and music lessons. After school, downtown sidewalks were packed with children carrying books and musical instruments. Shopkeepers often chatted with the youngsters as they stood outside their stores; children usually ran errands for their mothers. Mr. Biondi at the Sausage Factory would yell, "*Basta!*" 'Stop it!' when children buried their arms to their armpits in the big burlap bean sacks lined up outside his store on Second Avenue. The feel of the cool, smooth beans on the children's warm arms heated by Indian summer afternoons was worth the risk.

Social life in Valona centered around the family, work, social organizations, and church. At St. Rose of Lima Catholic Church, Sunday masses were always packed. After mass, everyone gathered outside the church to chat, often

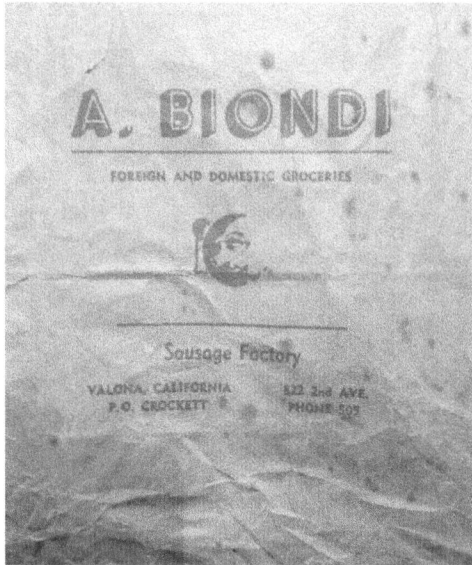

A bag from Biondi's Sausage Factory

in Italian, before going home to Sunday breakfast, lunch, or dinner with the extended family. Most classmates were Catholic, and children attended Catechism classes together. Mothers of friends, who were congregation members, usually taught the classes. Children memorized the *Baltimore Catechism*, reciting questions and answers over and over again and earning a tiny star for each question if answered correctly:

Question: "Who made us?"
Answer: "God made us."
Question: "Why did God make us?"
Answer: "God made us to show forth his goodness and to be happy with Him in heaven."

Many Catholic children made their First Holy Communion and Confirmation sacraments together. After these milestones, the children enjoyed a sit-down breakfast or celebrations in the church hall prepared by their proud mothers while their fathers stood to one side, watching the festivities, chatting, and smoking cigars. The parish nuns supervised

St. Cyril is pictured on the right

the religious education programs and were strict disciplinarians. Sister Cyril was probably the most formidable nun of them all. She buried her folded arms inside her habit, carrying a little wooden clicker, as the children called it. Children quickly fell to their knees when she clicked. This seems pretty funny now!

Given the variety of cultures in Crockett, many different religious festivals, such as the Portuguese Holy Ghost Festival, were celebrated with delicious food. After the parade, a big crowd gathered at the Community Auditorium to eat *soupish*, a 'traditional soup' cooked with meat and spices and served with sweet bread. The Sugar City festival was the highlight of the year. It included a parade with several marching bands, floats from Crockett's social organizations, clowns, old cars, a queen, and several contingents of horses. Always following the horses were the pooper scoopers, notable local men dressed like clowns, their antics meant to draw a laugh from the crowd. Fire trucks from the two local volunteer fire departments loaded with firefighters and their families started and ended the parade. Those riding on the trucks threw candy to the children lining the streets. After the parade, marching bands and drill teams, such as The Spanish Dons from Half Moon Bay, competed for prizes at the John Swett High School field. The day ended with an impressive fireworks show.

Parents knew each other and were involved with each other's children. In addition, the community supported its children's many activities and was proud of their accomplishments. Crockett's local newspaper, *The Crockett American*, reported on almost everything the children did, including publishing a list of names of those who had attended a birthday party, Camp Gold Hollow, the Camp Fire Camp, or Camp Wolfboro, the Boy Scout Camp.

An old Italian proverb was never more appropriate than in Crockett. It states, *Moglie e buoi dei paesi tuoi*, meaning 'it is best to marry someone from your hometown or country who understands and stays faithful to your traditions.' Because of its isolation, Crockett and Valona families often married each other, adding to the community's closeness. There was a rivalry between the towns of Crockett and Valona. Couples were teased if a Crockett young man crossed the line to marry a Valona young woman and vice versa.

Some people eat to live, but it is said that most Italians live to eat; that is, they are food-centric. For Italians, food signifies life's essential virtues: love, compassion, sharing, and kindness. It is also about community, family, friendship, art and tradition. Food is vital for leading a well-balanced life, mind (well-being), body (health), and spirit (peace and spirituality). Food is the defining factor for an Italian, the essence of life. As in most Italian-American communities across the United States, the memory of poverty and food scarcity suffered by the immigrants before coming to America necessitated *abbondanza*, 'abundance,' as the guiding principle at holiday tables. In some Italian-American families, the memory of scarcity is passed down from generation to generation. There is never enough food. Hence, a table covered with traditional seasonal food is mandatory for each holiday celebration.

∼

Anyone close to an Italian family knows that eating together has profound cultural significance. Bonds permeate the greater community when people from differing backgrounds share food regularly. Such was the case when a group of working women met regularly in the C&H Sugar refinery's women's locker room. Bringing their immigrant traditions to the refinery, they developed a camaraderie, an enduring bond when sharing their food and cake recipes over the years. It wasn't just their recipes that they shared; these women shared their celebrations, thoughts, lives, and cultural backgrounds that comprised the diversity of Crockett and California.

Chapter Five

Crockett's Golden Age

By the early 1940s, *Benessere*, C&H Sugar's industrial relations policy, had shaped the company and the town of Crockett. In a case study of C&H Sugar written by Boris Emmet, Ph.D. of the Stanford Graduate School of Business, Mr. Emmet described Crockett as a California model community, a utopia of sorts. Many residents of Crockett worked for C&H Sugar, where they were offered stable employment at livable wages, security, and a rich community environment focused on the arts and culture. Unbeknownst to most, whether they worked for C&H Sugar or not, they were experiencing Crockett's Golden Age.

During World War II, male workers were called up for military service, causing another labor shortage for C&H Sugar. At the height of the war, over seven hundred employees were away from the refinery, fighting in Europe and the South Pacific theatres. In addition, wages at the Kaiser Shipyards in Richmond and the Mare Island Naval Shipyard in Vallejo were higher, enticing male workers to leave the refinery. Since the early 1900s, women were offered limited gender-based job opportunities at the factory, including clerical positions, packing sugar, sewing sugar bags, working in the lab, and delivering mail. During the war, women assumed more responsibilities in the production department, as Rosie the Riveters did in the shipbuilding industry. Some in Crockett believe that the refinery survived the war years only because of the efforts of Crockett's hard-working, resourceful women.

When the men returned from the war, families focused on creating homes and a settled life for their children; life in Crockett remained quiet, modest, and provincial. As was the case throughout the United States, men who returned from the war wanted to put their war experiences behind them, live in peace, and move on with their lives. With so many employees living locally in Crockett, C&H Sugar continued its benevolent industrial relations policy, which benefited the company, the town, and its residents.

The collective immigration experiences of the Crockett and Valona residents gave rise to expectations that required generational support. Grandparents, parents, neighbors, and friends cooperated to help each family succeed. Every generation was expected to work hard, save money, limit spending, and build upon the economic progress made by the last generation. Italian families and friends worked together and helped each other succeed. Work parties where skills and labor were exchanged were common. Immigrant families and friends helped each other remodel or build houses on weekends to save money. Because Crockett and Valona were isolated communities within the San Francisco Bay Area, residents had time to devote to these projects, and many were skilled craftsmen and artisans. Instead of money changing hands, the barter system was the currency of the day. As with barn-raising in the Midwest, work parties were widespread throughout town. Building a new house was a family affair, and families were grateful for the help. While the men worked hard on the house, the women prepared and served hearty lunches, and young children spent the day happily playing at the construction site.

Teenage boys were given physically challenging laborers' tasks such as digging foundation footings and utility trenches. At the end of the weekend, many were sunburned and exhausted. Perhaps this hard physical work was an excellent way to teach young men that education and attending college could be a way to escape physical labor. Everyone anticipated the delicious alfresco lunch. Pasta, cold cuts, salad, fresh-baked bread, and tasty fruit pies were served on makeshift tables constructed from plywood sheets placed over sawhorses. Red wine and beer flowed freely, but not so much that the men couldn't swing their hammers after lunch. The children drank Kool-Aid served from festive ice-filled glass pitchers. After lunch, the women did the dishes and cleaned the construction site like laborers. There was something for everyone to do.

The refinery and its labor unions provided robust craft apprenticeships and journeyman programs, ensuring a continuous source of skilled craftsmen. Maintenance at the refinery was centralized to achieve greater efficiencies. Today, those services are outsourced. Crockett's skilled labor residents were the same as those in the refinery. These craftsmen included sheet metal workers, pipe fitters, boiler workers, carpenters, cement finishers, copper workers, machinists, painters, electricians, mechanics, brick masons, riggers, belting, and dock maintenance workers. C&H also had coopers on staff who made barrels from scratch. Local women with no opportunity to enjoy careers outside the home had the time and flexibility to care for the children, the sick, and the elderly. In contrast, another group of women worked at the refinery.

Children were oblivious to their unique environment, taking their lifestyle in Crockett for granted, having no idea they were experiencing Crockett's Golden Age. Despite the usual challenges of growing up in mid-twentieth century

California, life seemed idyllic. Children felt safe and could run free. They often played in similarly landscaped neighborhood gardens with beautiful spring and summer flowers, including purple irises, geraniums, calla lilies, and old roses of every variety and fragrance. Some houses had vacant flats downstairs where the children's grandmothers had once lived. Others had gardens with chicken coops or garden sheds perfect for playing house. Children were free to create make-believe fantasies, acting them out daily. Like the creative playgrounds found in Scandinavia, play structures such as tree houses were built out of scavenged scrap lumber. Since Crockett was a blue-collar community with many craftsmen and ongoing home construction projects, there was an ample supply of tools and building materials. One fort was named Fort Ash because it was built in a large ash tree in a backyard on Lillian Street. It was elaborate, with a sturdy ladder to reach the platform where its builders could enjoy snacks and lunches. It had a view of the Carquinez Straits and, of course, of the refinery. In its honor, a flag was made by the mothers embroidered with its name. The flag was proudly flown all summer long.

Without TVs, computers, or cell phones to steal their attention, children had time to be creative, busy, or bored. With little discretionary income to spend on vacations, mass transit options, freeways, or comfortable cars, summers often were spent in town or at Bay Area destinations a short distance away. Parents encouraged their children to go outdoors when the sun was shining, and the sun shone in Crockett just about every summer day. When not swimming at the Crockett Club or participating in C&H Sugar-sponsored recreational activities, Crockett children, with their friends and classmates, hiked into the hills above Valona to white barns, a local farmer's big barn. They played as cowboys or cowgirls, Indians, or army soldiers in shady oak-filled gullies. With helmets and authentic United States Army gear their fathers had brought home after World War II, elaborate battles took place in the hills. Clumps of green grass with a big ball of wet soil still intact, pretend bombs, were lobbed from one front line to the next. When it was exceptionally windy in March, gangs of children flew kites. So many kites crashed and broke that parents stopped giving their children money to buy new ones at the five-and-dime store. Instead, they taught them how to make their own — flying them with string left over from the refinery. After spring rains, children careened down steep, wet, grassy slopes on flattened cardboard boxes. In summer, they got into mischief stealing ripe fruit and having fruit fights in the middle of Lillian Street, just above the Soda Works warehouse. During the Halloween evening parade, groups of teenagers threw overripe tomatoes and rotten eggs at the John Swett High School marching band, hiding amongst the foliage on the hill above the intersection of Rolph Park and Pomona Street so as not to be caught.

A favorite destination for local children was Pete's Ranch. Now a part of the Carquinez Strait Regional Shoreline, it was once a working ranch owned by Pete Sanna. Pete co-managed the Sanna & Maretti Creamery, which was built on the grounds of the old Murphy Ranch property; it was commonplace for local parents and their children to visit the ranch to feed the horses and occasionally watch cowboys herding and branding cattle. The cowboys wore long-sleeved western shirts, cowboy boots, and hats. On branding days, a lot of action happened. In the corral, adept, rough-and-tumble cowboys shoved branding irons into the

Pete's Ranch, formerly the Sanna & Maretti Creamery

red-hot coals of a corral fire. They waited for the irons to reach the perfect temperature to burn Pete's ranch brand onto the calves' hindquarters. The calves were held

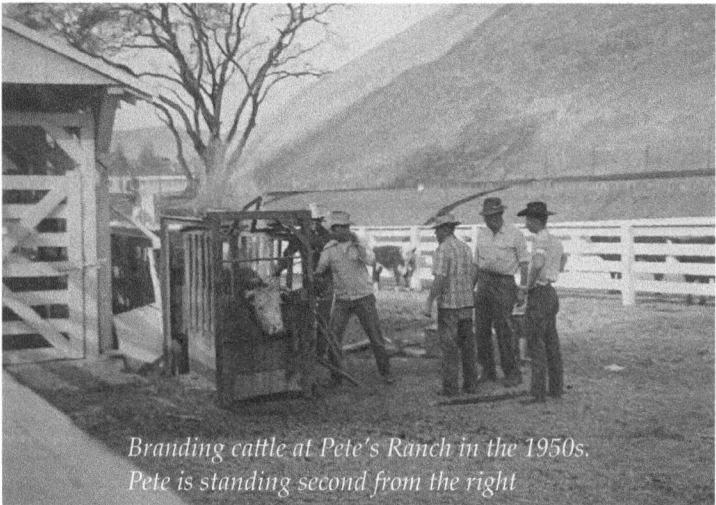

Branding cattle at Pete's Ranch in the 1950s. Pete is standing second from the right

immobile in the shoot while steam rose from the fresh wounds of the calves, crying in pain. Today, only the house, original barn, and milk house remain.

C&H Sugar was the most significant supporter of community culture and events and actively promoted Crockett's arts. For example, when the Annual Art and Garden Show was held in the spring, everyone, including refinery management and workers, was encouraged to participate. Artwork entries of all types, including oil paintings, pastels, and watercolors, were beautifully displayed. Floral arrangements with flowers grown in Crockett gardens were showcased, including exceptional displays of fragrant old roses, bearded irises, and calla lilies. The company supported the

Annual Art and Garden Show
held in the Crockett Club gym

creation of beautiful gardens by maintaining the Public Planting Program to beautify Crockett. Flowers, trees, and shrubs, propagated by a staff of twenty-two C&H Sugar gardeners in a large greenhouse, were offered to residents free of charge.

An extensive summer recreation program for all Crockett children was housed in crafts cottages and unused old temporary housing initially built for C&H Sugar employees in what is now the John Swett High School field. The program was directed by Mrs. Blanch Ball and her staff of leaders and teenage volunteers. Mrs. Ball was always smiling and cheerful, dressed as if on safari, in khaki Bermuda shorts, a belt,

Room for Play

ALL CROCKETT BOYS AND GIRLS HAVE SPACE AND MEANS TO GROW AND PLAY

SUPERVISED fun for the boys and girls of Crockett is available in unlimited quantities twelve months out of the year at the community playground located on Loring Avenue south of the Crockett Club.

In any average day about 200 boys and girls will make use of the recreation facilities provided by the playground.

Total attendance last year at the playground amounted to about 75,000. More than a hundred types of recreation are provided by the playground each year. Not all of these

The crafts cottage offered handicrafts, photography, and woodworking. Making puppets and holding puppet shows was a popular activity

a white shirt, and sensible shoes. Summer offerings included a playground, a woodworking shop, a photography dark-room, a puppet theater, painting and ceramics studios, a canteen with a jukebox, television, and a shuffleboard court. There was something for everyone. Sports teams, tennis, and archery were offered for athletic children. There were classes in drama, basket weaving, jewelry making, baton twirling, flag drills, and homemaking for those less so. Trips

On September 13, 1952, over 200 Crockett children attended the Annual Pet Show

to the zoo and baseball games rounded out the curriculum. The recreation program was year-round, but the summer program was so extensive and diverse that it ensured Crockett's youth would never be bored. A summer reading program at the library also made for a busy summer. Mrs. Ball also directed the Culture Club, organizing cultural trips and activities for adults who enjoyed sports teams, games, and a concert band.

The Annual Pet Show held in the tiny Library Park on Loring Avenue was a much-anticipated event. The park, adjacent to the library, was across the street from the train station and next to Hite's Drug Store. At the September 1952 show, approximately 200 Crockett children and a large crowd of spectators attended. Whoever organized this event indeed had a great sense of humor; sixty ribbons were awarded in many categories, including a ribbon awarded to the dog that wagged the longest tail.

Perhaps the most memorable event in town was the annual Christmas Play, sponsored by C&H Sugar and performed by local children at the John Swett High School Auditorium. The company also sponsored a Christmas dance for adults. At the end of the play, the large doors between the auditorium and arcade opened, and the children rushed in. Toys for every child in Crockett and employees' children living out of town were piled high on tables. Santa Claus presided, and each child received a gender-specific and age-appropriate gift: pink caramel popcorn and a red mesh Christmas stocking. The stocking was filled with small toys, sweets, and a gingerbread cookie topped with a Victorian-style Santa Claus sugar transfer. Those who performed in the play received a box of See's candy.

Lodena Edgecumbe, a dance teacher from Vallejo who also

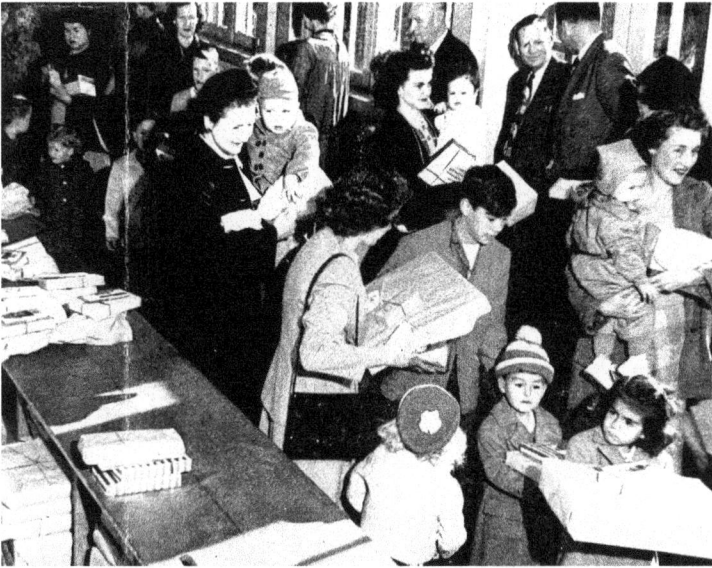

Toy giveaway after the Christmas Play

taught ballet classes at the Crockett Club, was hired by the company to choreograph, audition, and train local children to perform at the Christmas Play. Lodena was thin, petite, and sophisticated. She was the epitome of a ballerina. Her hair was pulled severely into a bun, and she wore a black leotard and black ballet slippers with black elastic that held them snug to her tiny feet. Little did the children know that Lodena had a story all her own. She had been discovered as an infant alone on a San Francisco Bay ferry after surviving the 1906 San Francisco earthquake and fire. Her birth parents were presumed dead and were never identified. The Edgecumbe family of Vallejo adopted her. As a little girl, Lodena studied dance. In 1915, she performed at the Panama-Pacific International Exposition in San Francisco. She performed in vaudeville, toured the United States, Mexico, and Europe with the

Pavley-Oukrainsky dance troupe, and danced in the Chicago and Manhattan Opera Companies. In Lodina's later life, she directed a troupe of young women dancers in Vallejo, inspired by Isadora Duncan, the famed American dancer who performed throughout Europe and the United States.

The Nutcracker Suite dolls

Every child in Crockett dreamed of being in the Christmas Play because it was glittery, magical, and overflowing with the Christmas spirit. Professional pianists played at after-school rehearsals, and a professional orchestra played at the dress rehearsal and all performances. The John Swett High School Auditorium, with its exceptional acoustics, was bursting with deep, rich symphonic sound. The Nutcracker Suite overture was thrilling in this space. Added to the spectacular music were the decorations. Natural spruce garlands adorned the entrances to the auditorium, and doors were hung with wreaths, their scent adding to the atmosphere. Professionally designed stage sets built in the refinery's

Carpenter Shop Staff

Carpenter Shop were painted by the Paint Shop. The lighting, beautiful costumes, and theatrical makeup all heightened the atmosphere.

Everyone in town dressed in their Sunday best for the performances. It was traditional for Crockett women to

The John Swett Auditorium was adorned with fresh spruce garlands. Note Santa guarding the doors to the arcade that would open at the end of the performance. Behind the doors, gifts were piled high for all Crockett's children.

create for the play unique Christmas corsages made of flocked plastic bells with glittered edges, floral wire, holly leaves, and bright red metal bells. If not made at home, residents could purchase a corsage for fifteen cents at the Sprouse Rietz five and dime store on the corner of Pomona and Second Streets on the way to the performance.

Crockett and Valona were home to several notable citizens during this Golden Age. In 1950, the famous Hollywood movie star Aldo Ray was elected town constable before Hollywood talent scouts discovered him. His big start in Hollywood began when he drove his brother to an audition at a movie company's casting call in Vallejo, California. When the agents heard Aldo's raspy voice, they asked him to do a screen test. Thus, Aldo's film career began. He worked with Spencer Tracy and Katharine Hepburn in *Pat and Mike*. Subsequently, he received a Golden Globe nomination for this role along with Richard Burton

Aldo Ray

and Robert Wagner. Aldo starred in films such as *The Marrying Kind*, *Let's Do It Again*, and *Battle Cry*. He was often cast as a tough guy.

Aldo's mother, Maria, was a noteworthy cook and baker in town. Maria was a typical Italian mamma, short, stout, and sturdy. She wore a full apron with her long hair pulled back into a tight bun. Maria had a spunky attitude, a hearty laugh, and a smile that lit up her whole face, eyes closed. Maria once brought a plate of her famous cream cheese cookies to a Weight Watchers meeting, prioritizing her sense of Italian hospitality and the importance of sharing food with others over losing weight.

Dr. Sam Eldridge was Crockett's memorable small-town doctor and a local legend. A graduate of Stanford University, his office was across the street from Imerone's Bakery on Second Avenue. Everyone in town has a story about Dr. Sam. Always gruff and to the point, he liked to cuss at one's illness or injury and draw a picture of the ailment on the paper that covered the exam table. He gave painful shots, made house calls, and was so compassionate he was known to sit through the night with a sick child. Generous, Dr. Sam gave free exams to local sports teams and volunteer firefighters. Dr. Sam Eldridge died at 69 in 1972 as Crockett's Golden Age faded. The Carquinez Women's Club still awards annual scholarships in his name.

Jim Turner was a local sports legend. He was a placekicker in the American Football League (AFL) and the National Football League (NFL). He played for the Denver Broncos and the New York Jets, where he played a crucial role in winning Super Bowl III on January 12, 1969, in Miami, Florida. Jim received many awards during his career. Still, perhaps he is remembered most in Crockett for his loyalty and devotion to his hometown and its youth. Jim passed away on June 10, 2023.

Crockett offered several informal meeting places for residents around town. These included the post office on Rolph Park, Pedrotti Hardware on Second Avenue, Crockett's several gas stations, and its diners, including the "Dog House" and the "Chat & Chew." Larry Pedrotti was a tremendous resource for do-it-yourself projects around the house. Not only did he share his knowledge freely, but he and his brother, Al Vaio, experts at stocking their small store, always seemed to have just what was needed to complete a project. Ray Rodgers, Jim Grady, or any of the Desmond Brothers were always present at their gas stations for a quick chat or a lengthy conversation full of life advice for young people. There wasn't an issue they couldn't solve. The Dog House was a favorite meeting place for high school students in the days of bobby socks, oxfords, and poodle skirts.

~

And the party went on! It is unlikely that George Morrison Rolph could have anticipated the positive consequences of his progressive industrial relations policy, *Benessere*, the catalyst for creating what has been referred to as Crockett's Golden Age. Nor could he have imagined the negative impact on Crockett and its immigrant neighborhood, Valona, decades later, when the construction of access to Highway 4 and the building of Interstate 80 ended Crockett's isolation. Parallel with these developments, the company abandoned *Benessere* under industry pressures and the demographic changes that arose in the mid-twentieth century. Crockett's Golden Age was coming to a close.

Chapter Six
Unexpected Forces Drive Change

In the mid-1950s, village life in Valona changed dramatically when approximately 150 homes were moved or torn down to make way for the construction of Highway 80 and the second eastbound bridge. The enormous excavation, or cut, as it was called, removed 9,000,000 cubic yards of dirt and a portion of Valona's heart and soul. The State of California exercised its right to seize private property through eminent domain at costs many in Crockett felt were below market value. Italian immigrants and their first-generation children didn't know they could fight for a better financial settlement, nor how to do it. There was no legal infrastructure, such as legal aid, to help them, and families suffered financially. Faustino Pagni worked diligently, but unsuccessfully, to convince state engineers to adopt a less direct route to the bridge to save Valona, and many Valona families had to move out of town. Valona lost much of its core as families moved to Rodeo, Martinez, Vallejo, and Benicia. Crockett's population diminished from a high of 5,000 residents to what it is today, approximately 3,300. Local businesses began to suffer as almost a third of the population was lost. Crockett and Valona couldn't sustain local businesses.

Crockett became less isolated due to all the new roads in the area. The new Interstate 80 freeway brought traffic from the west and east, replacing antiquated Highway 40 as the only major route to Crockett. The Cummings Skyway improved access to Highway 4. This new road reduced drive times to cities such as Martinez, Concord, Walnut Creek,

Oblivious to what the new interstate freeway would mean for Crockett and Valona, children enjoyed playing in the destruction around them.

View from Wanda and Second Avenue towards the big cut and rising piers.

and all points east. The new roads made it easier for Crockett residents to leave town to shop and for entertainment. Malls and discount stores developed in adjacent larger communities, and many small businesses in Crockett started closing as residents shopped elsewhere for novelty, lower prices, and variety. The community had an appetite for newness—new buildings and new experiences.

Valona's children were oblivious to how the new freeway might affect the community or how modern life would intrude into their peaceful existence. On summer nights, after dinner, when the men excavating the highway had left for the day, children excitedly played on the construction equipment, pretending to drive massive D9 Caterpillar tractors. They climbed upon and jumped from the enormous tires of the carryalls that hauled the dirt away from the big cut. The excavation equipment smelled like dirt mixed with

View towards Pomona Street

Pomona and Sixth Streets

oil and diesel fuel. The children gleefully played with their friends in the abandoned houses that giant cranes would soon destroy. The cranes were fitted with massive wrecking balls that crushed the buildings, rendering them into a pile of rubble, sending dust clouds aloft. Valona looked like a war zone or as if a tornado had passed through town. Close by, explosions rocked the hills as dynamite was used to blast away rocks, enabling tons of soil removal. Children hunted for fossils unearthed by the dynamite, some bringing them to the University of California at Berkeley for identification by the Geology Department.

Several residents' fears were realized when the project was completed. The new freeway was so close to some homes that residents could hear big rig drivers shifting gears, the engine's compression echoing as the trucks glided down the sloped roadway as they approached the bridge. Valona's quiet life was disrupted forever.

Today, two parallel bridges hold the massive volume of vehicles traveling on Interstate 80 over the Carquinez Straits to destinations east and west. The eastbound bridge, now called the old bridge by residents, was completed in 1958. The original westbound bridge, which no longer exists, was completed in 1927, two years before the Garden City Ferry's retirement. The span was the first major crossing of San Francisco Bay. It opened on May 21, 1927, the same day Charles Lindbergh landed his plane, the Spirit of St. Louis, at Le Bourget Field in Paris, the world's first solo nonstop transatlantic flight between New York and Paris. Some elderly residents recalled attending the bridge's dedication ceremony. They shared vivid memories of walking across the bridge and eating five-cent hot dogs when they reached the Vallejo side.

Carquinez Bridge Opening Day — the same day Charles Lindbergh accomplished his solo flight across the Atlantic Ocean from New York to Paris.

*Dedication Ceremony
for the original bridge*

In 2003, a new westbound bridge replaced the original. The Alfred Zampa Memorial Bridge is dedicated to a local ironworker, the son of Italian immigrants and the patriarch of a local family. Mr. Zampa had worked on the Oakland-San Francisco Bay Bridge and the Golden Gate Bridge. He is a local legend because he fell from the Golden Gate Bridge during its construction and lived to tell the tale. As the only bridge named for a worker in the United States, it pays tribute to the men and women who work in the construction trades on such monumental projects. It is appropriate that this honor should be bestowed on Crockett with its secure blue-collar foundation.

Another devastating loss to Crockett was an electrical fire at the old St. Rose of Lima Catholic Church in 1963. The fire was limited to the sacristy behind the altar, but church elders, thinking that a larger church was necessary to accommodate future growth in Crockett, pushed to tear the old church down. The old heritage building was demolished,

Interior, St. Rose of Lima Catholic Church,
lost to a fire in the mid-1960s

creating a new, modern, generic replacement structure across the street, an excellent example of the progressive culture of the 1960s. Everything had to be new and contemporary,—"Out with the old and in with the new." The beautiful vintage church with its altar, reminiscent of St. Teresa's Catholic Church in Bodega Bay, was demolished. St. Rose lost its stunning stained glass windows, old Italian crystal chandeliers, and the Archangel Gabriel fresco painted high above the altar on the left.

Residents felt a sense of sadness, loss, and unease each time another store closed its doors. The old ways were changing, but not for the better. An essential part of the community was vanishing. At one time, children could walk home from catechism class at St. Rose and stop by Imerone's Bakery for a small bag of candy. Candy was weighed on a big brass candy scale to the left of the blue front doors. Behind the candy

Imerone's Bakery, Valona, California

counter was a uniformed, patient sales lady with a big
smile and a cheerful greeting. The bakery cases were filled
with cakes, brioche, and Danish pastries called butter
horns and snails by the locals. The sales ladies placed the
pastries in a pink pastry box, separating the pastries with

Vintage Imerone's Bakery Sticker

tiny square tissues. The boxes were tied with baker's twine, making it easy to carry them home.

Behind the cases, photographs of wedding cakes made for local couples were proudly displayed on the shelves, showcasing the bakers' artistry. Displayed along with the cakes were traditional Italian-style wedding favors, *bomboniere*. Just as one would find in Italy, the *bomboniere*, small packets of five candied Jordan almonds, called *confetti*, were encased in bridal veil netting. Five almonds signified wishes for the couple: health, wealth, happiness, fertility, and long life. The almonds were tied with satin ribbon into various shapes, including small packets or flowers. A tiny label tied to the ribbon displayed the bride and groom's names and wedding dates.

Crockett and Valona were walkable communities, and a driver's license wasn't required. With the loss of local stores during the late 1950s and 60s, residents who didn't drive had to rely on family and friends to drive them out of town to shop. Their only other option was to take the Greyhound Bus, which regularly stopped in Crockett on Pomona Street directly below Highway 80. It was convenient to take the Greyhound to Vallejo, which had a modern bus station blocks from the central business district that offered all types of stores, including two large department stores.

For nearly half a century, Crockett residents heard a woman saying, "Number please," when making a telephone call. All communities in California except Crockett and the town of Avalon on Catalina Island had rotary dial phones. Crockett's manual switchboard, located in the telephone building at the corner of Rolph Park and Winslow Streets, was staffed by thirty-four women operators around the clock. The operators matched plugs to chords to complete calls.

*Crockett's telephone operators
in the late 1960s*

Party lines were frequent with numbers such as 975J. Hearing another conversation already in progress, residents were instructed to hang up the phone quickly, but sometimes the temptation was too great, and calls weren't always private. It's no wonder everyone in town knew each other's business. Upgrading to a private line resulted in a phone number, such as 297. Imagine how hard it was to call home from anywhere other than within Crockett. It wasn't unusual for a caller to have to summon the operator and convince her to place the call because a three-digit number couldn't be dialed from a rotary dial phone. The explanation seemed far-fetched and more like a prank.

An example of how this system impacted local businesses is Pagni Construction Company, which employed several Crockett residents. Pagni Construction built large schools such as Carondelet and De La Salle High Schools in Concord and the U.C. Davis Veterinary Hospital. Estimating a project's cost was a manual process, and sharp pencils and ledger paper were used to document bids received by telephone from sub-contractors. Without computers, there were many opportunities to make errors. Staff and family members manned the telephones on bid day. Since Crockett still had party lines, the operators had to stay alert to facilitate all those calls, resulting in the operators playing a critical role on multiple bid days throughout the year. Pagni Construction delivered beautifully wrapped gifts to the telephone operators at Christmas to thank them for their support. Dr. Sam did the same. On November 15, 1969,

Cartoon from a Cubelet Press article reporting on the demise of Crockett's antiquated phone system

Crockett's telephone system was finally upgraded to an automated system, and rotary dial phones became the norm. Crockett's telephone operators lost their jobs or moved on to other assignments, while Crockett lost another unique piece of its past.

Another relic lost to the past was the refinery's industrial steam whistle. The whistle blew at least seven times every day, without fail, seven days a week: at 7:55 a.m. to alert workers that the day shift was about to begin; at 8:00 a.m., the start of a new shift; 12:00 p.m., lunch; 12:25 p.m., five-minute warning before the end of lunch; 12:30, the end of lunch; 4:00 p.m., shift change for the production department; and 4:30 end of the shift for office and management staff. The whistle, reminiscent of a train whistle on steroids, was integral to Crockett's safety net and sense of security. Hearing the whistle blow on a regular schedule was not unlike hearing the familiar rhythmic sounds of a stately grandfather's clock. Mothers often told their children to come home when a particular whistle blew. Since the whistle blew frequently, their children weren't away from home for very long.

The whistle was essential to Crockett and Valona's fire departments. It blew two or three-digit numbers correlated to a specific area in town to guide the volunteer fire department's response. Every resident had a list of the codes and their corresponding locations for quick reference. Hearing the unique whistle, firefighters ran from their houses, jumped into their cars, and headed to the fire station in either Valona or Crockett. Hearing the whistle, neighborhood dogs bayed in accompaniment. The whistle also alerted the volunteer fire department to a mutual aid fire in another community or a general emergency by continuously blowing the number four. When the crisis ended, an all-clear signal blew, and everyone relaxed.

The whistle could be frightening, especially when it

blew the number for one's neighborhood, causing residents to worry that their houses were on fire. During the 1950s, in the Cold War years following World War II, yearly Civil Defense air-raid drills were held at Carquinez Grammar School. The whistle blew nonstop, and students had to shelter under their desks until the all-clear signal was heard. Children felt as if the drill would last an eternity. Many children whose fathers had fought during World War II had heard wartime stories, such as how their fathers' unit had been strafed by enemy planes in New Guinea. Most had seen footage on television showing the attack on Pearl Harbor and the Blitz. These stories and images caused the children's imaginations to run wild during the air raid drills. It wasn't too far-fetched for them to imagine war planes flying in formation from west to east over Crockett, positioned to drop bombs at any moment. It was terrifying for some of the children. Around the year 2000, the whistle was silenced as the fire department no longer needed it, and after several new residents complained about the noise.

The refinery's workforce began to dwindle in response to industry cost pressures and automation. In the 1930s, when the refinery employed more than 2,000 workers, 90 percent of the refinery's workforce lived in town. By 1960, less than half of its employees were residents. Today, in 2023, the refinery produces more than six million pounds of sugar daily, employing more than 450 people. Only a handful of employees live in Crockett and Valona. Due to these demographic changes and industry pressures, the cost of C&H Sugar's benevolence, *Benessere*, could no longer be sustained, and the refinery began to operate like most American industries, somewhat detached from its community. But it wasn't easy for Crockett residents and employees to give up on *Benessere* and the bonds and connections it had created. And more changes were to come.

The Crockett Club, the beloved institution housing the local swimming pools and many recreational activities, closed on December 31, 1965. It was torn down to make a parking lot, bringing to mind Joni Mitchell's song lyrics, "They paved Paradise and put up a parking lot." Additional parking spaces were needed as more employees from surrounding communities drove to work. Ironically, the new community swimming pool was built on a portion of Alexander Park dedicated to George Morrison Rolph's memory. A good part of the park's gardens were destroyed.

As if in the grip of a strong California earthquake, Crockett was shaken to its core by these changes and was forced to transition and find a way forward. However, *Benessere* was deeply rooted in Crockett citizens' hearts and souls. The remaining parks and buildings that residents passed daily were reminders of the shared values and culture created decades before by George Morrison Rolph and C&H Sugar. These roots shaped a sense of civic responsibility, just as Crockett's forefathers had hoped.

Created more than fifty years ago, the Crockett Improvement Association began to work diligently on Crockett's behalf. Because Crockett remains an unincorporated township of Contra Costa County, a Citizen's Advisory Committee was formed to work with the County on shared interests. In the mid-1970s, this small group of active citizens raised approximately $300,000, enough money to save the Community Auditorium from demolition. The Committee worked with Contra Costa County to assume the Auditorium's management and led a renovation effort. In 2006,

Contra Costa County returned the Auditorium, now called the Community Center, to the District and local control. Hence, the Crockett Recreation Department manages, improves, and beautifully maintains the Community Center with the Crockett Community Foundation's support.

Although C&H Sugar started to reduce its benevolent community programs, it still offered its employees secure employment, a pension, and healthcare benefits. Long embued with the spirit of *Benessere*, Crockett's citizens stepped up. With a passion for their town, they began moving a new Crockett forward with energy inspired by their memories of what had been. Volunteerism flourished. This is an appropriate example of Margaret Mead's famous remark: "Never doubt that a small group of thoughtful, committed citizens can change the world: indeed, it's the only thing that ever has."

Since many of Crockett's residents were immigrants or their descendants, the refinery remained central to many families. *Benessere*, community well-being, and the sense of broader community have endured. With the region's emphasis on a robust and unspoken bond between family life and community life, its shared values and cultural traditions have remained unshaken and intact.

$\sim$

With all the destruction, loss, and churning, Crockett was catapulted into the modern culture of the San Francisco Bay Area and California, leaving many Crockett residents yearning for what had been. Even as the roads and bridges to Crockett have flourished and allowed some residents to leave and others to come to replace them, and as C&H Sugar has evolved into a more efficient version of its previous self, the history of this unique community and the bonds created over the years are its legacy and live on.

Part 2

Working at the Refinery

Chapter Seven
Breaking the Sugar Ceiling

In April 1966, James Brown recorded *It's a Man's Man's Man's Man's World*, a song whose title and lyrics shared his opinion that women in society were powerless. Indeed, in 1966, there were few career opportunities for women except in typical female roles such as nursing, teaching, or secretarial work. Women were expected to fulfill their traditional roles as wives and mothers. The title was also apropos of the benefit C&H Sugar extended to college-bound young men, sons of employees, by offering summer jobs at excellent wages. The philanthropic program was a significant remnant of *Benessere*, and it was mutually beneficial to the refinery as it supplied flexible, temporary workers to cover for those permanent employees taking extended vacations. Appropriate to the time, this generous benefit wasn't offered to college-bound young women. At the request of employees with college-bound daughters, in the summer of 1966, C&H Sugar expanded the program, enabling this generation of young women to *break the sugar ceiling*. With the same opportunities as their male counterparts, young women could earn enough money to pay for one year at university, including tuition, room and board, and books.

For these young women, their first day working at the refinery was both thrilling and stressful. Indeed, the experience contrasted with the predictability of high school; they were out of their comfort zone. But what unique experiences would the refinery offer? Could the young women withstand the working conditions at the refinery?

Could they do the job? So much was at stake.

Approaching the refinery's main gate on Loring Avenue, Barbara, one of the new summer hires, had butterflies in her stomach. Classically designed, the impressive vintage main

C&H Sugar's Main Gate on Loring Avenue

entrance fronted the vintage two-story building constructed with durable materials, red brick, and concrete, with windows trimmed in wood. The building's design elements were gracefully proportioned, balanced, and symmetrically placed, including moldings, cornices, windows, planters, and doors. In the background, the multi-storied tall, dark, stately brick refinery was the perfect expression of a factory built in the late 19th century. To the right of the main building, the refinery's towering smokestack tapered to an elaborate black decoration at the top. The refinery was noisy, and plumes of steam rose from the numerous valves on its roof into the deep blue sky. It seemed as if the refinery was alive!

Elegantly polished brass doors that seemed to signify pride of place and security signaled the refinery's gateway

*The C&H Sugar Refinery
as seen from Loring Avenue*

to employees and visitors. Inside, the walls were paneled in oak, stained a dark black walnut color, with the ornate cornices, trims, and moldings one would expect to find in a stately, classically designed building. The terrazzo floors gleamed with a fresh coat of sealer and wax. Those entering felt the coolness of the space and inhaled their first scent of molasses. It was then that Barbara realized she was about to experience industrialized America firsthand.

George, the C&H Sugar security guard, waved and smiled from the guard station positioned in the center of the space. The guards wore uniforms, hats, and guns and functioned as a police force in and around the refinery. Crockett's children knew they could always count on the C&H cops, as they were called. George's nickname was Pinky. Children were fascinated by Pinky's large, silver, holstered revolver. He wore his gun on his hip and was always happy to show it off.

Barbara walked timidly to the timecard station, a vertical rack with a unique clock attached to the wall just before the footbridge to the refinery, and punched in like all employees. Excitedly, she had officially started her first day of work, earning the precious money she needed to sustain herself through a year of college. Alleluia!

Crossing the footbridge over the train tracks, the air changing from cool and crisp to warm and heavy. Sticky and gooey, the air was laden with moisture, sugar, and the intense aroma of molasses. Veteran female employees were elegantly dressed as if they were going to work at a San Francisco office. They wore skirts or dresses, colorful silk scarves tied around their necks, nylons with high heels, and costume jewelry. All the women, young or veteran, were on their way to the women's locker room on the fourth floor. Angelo, a jovial member of Veterans of Foreign Wars and an usher at St. Rose of Lima Catholic Church, operated the elevator and greeted everyone warmly. Soon, he would have everyone in the elevator laughing–a great way to start the day.

At their assigned lockers in the women's locker room, the young women found everyone and everything they needed to make their summer at the refinery a success. Meeting the veteran women, the young hires were introduced to and inducted into the sisterhood among the veteran working women. Sisterhood naturally developed among women who lived in the same community and worked together over the years. Their sisterhood was essential to the community's life and the refinery's unique culture. Their bond was the kind of virtue that bound the community together and would affect future generations.

Their welcome was so warm that some felt flushed and embarrassed. The young women were such a novelty that

The "sisters" in the Women's Locker Room

veteran women gathered around the new hires at their lockers and began to orient them informally. Many of the sisters were local friends and neighbors. There were Mamie, Louise, Mildred, Pearl, Rose, Rita, Jo, Kay, Josie, Mary, Liz, and Connie, to name a few. The veteran women laughed, carried on, and showed the young women the ropes. This process would continue all summer. The new hires were asked many questions, such as, "How are your parents?" "How was graduation?" "Are you excited?" What are your plans for college?" The atmosphere was festive. The veterans assured the young women they would do fine and said they were eager to help. The animated crowd continued to gather, but the young women had to dress quickly and begin their first work assignments. The two groups of women, new and veterans, would have opportunities to get to know each other even better as the summer went on.

Many veteran women were immigrants, and others were first-generation immigrant daughters. Some veterans were single, working to support themselves; others were married, bucking the trend to work outside the home to support their families. A few had migrated from Mexico, the Midwest, or the Dust Bowl. For all this diversity, the women shared a tight bond of friendship, a sisterhood, at the refinery. Many sisters had worked together for more than three decades and had labored side by side through the Depression and World War II. They had experienced fear, scarcity, and challenges but had supported each other during those troublesome times. Since only a small percentage of the total number of factory employees were women, the locker room had become their clubhouse, a place of respite. In this Golden Age in Crockett, they shared the ups and downs of life, their traditions, cultures, food, celebrations, and the everyday simplicity and routine of lunches, breaks, and work. And they shared their delicious cakes and their recipes!

Like her high school male classmates who joined her at the refinery for the summer, Barbara felt privileged to have this summer job so close to home. At one time, C&H Sugar's summer hires included over 125 college students who worked in all refinery areas and covered for regular employees enjoying their three and four-week vacations. However, Barbara had to wear a uniform, unlike the young men who could dress casually in jeans and t-shirts. On the wooden benches outside her locker, Barbara found three starched white cotton uniforms in her appropriate dress size, enough to get her through an entire work cycle of ten days until shutdown. Since it was hot inside the refinery, Barbara would sweat from the heat and physical labor. She worried about whether she could tolerate excessive heat and dehydration.

Clementina Pagni in an early 1940s version of a C&H Sugar uniform

The uniform, made of heavy white cotton broadcloth, had cap sleeves, a collar, a cinched waist, and a wrap-around A-line skirt. An ample breast pocket on the left provided room for a colorful cotton-printed handkerchief. Many veteran women stiffly starched and ironed these hankies into the shape of a fan, making the folds precise and crisp. Some sprayed the hankies with perfume. The hankies could be purchased at the Sprouse and Rietz dime store or the Valona Emporium and were available in various designs and colors to match the seasons. The uniform and handkerchief were reminiscent of those diner waitresses wore in old movies.

The uniform included comfortable white nursing shoes and a hairnet, which posed a problem. In the late sixties, the style was big hair, or a hair hat, as it was called. Hair was teased by backcombing to establish height, smoothed with a comb, and then secured with hair spray. The hairnet deflated

*Friends working at the refinery. Those not
in uniform had non-sugar-production jobs.*

one's hair, smashing it close to the head. Wearing it with the
uniform made Barbara feel self-conscious and out of style.

After dressing, the young women were given a short tour
of the locker room's dining area. Numerous sofas, covered
in glossy moss green Naugahyde, a tough vinyl fabric that
could withstand a refinery's abuse, lined the walls. Though
they didn't know it initially, the sofas would soon become
their best friends.

An impressive bank of large windows on one locker
room wall faced the Carquinez Straits. The women enjoyed
the view out of these windows every day. In lost moments,
Barbara daydreamed about being aboard one of the sail-
boats sailing by, likely headed for the California Delta's
fresh, calm waters, reminding the viewer of refreshing recreation. Barbara thought about the lazy days of summers past

when she spent her afternoons swimming with friends at the Crockett Club. Still, she had to stay focused and remain grateful for this job.

The swift maneuvers of river patrol boats could be seen on the straits. The quick watercraft were constructed at the Mare Island Naval Shipyard in Vallejo and tested on San Pablo Bay and the Carquinez Straits for future deployment in Vietnam. Barbara thought about the future of her male high school friends, many of whom were headed for that controversial, deadly war. She felt grateful to have been born a woman. At the same time, she felt guilty.

During coffee breaks and lunch, the women workmates gathered at the rectangular laminate-topped tables in the locker room's dining area. Several newspapers and magazines were scattered about on the tables. Sizeable pink bakery boxes full of donuts, plates of cookies, and delicious homemade cakes were displayed on the tables for everyone to eat. A large refrigerator stood in the corner to store workers' lunches. On the counters were several large pots brewing coffee. Caffeine was essential to fight the monotony workers felt working on a production line and to remain awake.

Several areas around the room held carefully arranged personal items reserved for different groups. The young women quickly learned that one of the rules of the road was to respect the domain of each group and not intrude on anyone's space. Several handwork projects, including knitting, embroidery, and crochet, waited for their owners to return at break or lunchtime. Some crochet projects were made with the refinery's discarded cotton thread.

The candy vending machine was a favorite item in the locker room. It offered favorite candy bars, such as a PayDay, whose name's significance was not lost on the young hires.

After two weeks, with the refinery's heat and the physicality of the work, Barbara began to lose so much weight that eating a whole PayDay became an earned extravagance and indulgence. The pleasure of eating a sweet, gooey, nutty, salty, caramel, and peanut candy bar late into any shift, including the graveyard shift, can't be overstated.

After their quick orientation in the locker room and changing into their uniform, veteran sisters took the young recruits into the inner depths of the refinery. Exiting the locker room, they encountered the refinery's wall of heat and humidity, leaving many breathless. They experienced a more intense warmth than they felt on the footbridge. A not-unpleasant sugary and molasses aroma filled the refinery's air. Barbara could feel the heat and dampness in her throat, and it was then that she realized she would have to adapt to this new industrial environment.

The man-lift, a vertical conveyor belt that transported

C&H Sugar mechanics repairing the man lift

men and women in pants (women who delivered mail) to floors above and below, could be seen but not used by women in dresses or skirts. Footholds and grab bars at chest height, regularly positioned along the belt's length, passed through holes in several refinery floors and ceilings. A low handrail around the hole in the floor created a barrier protecting riders from falling through to the floor below. Stepping onto a foothold, riders reached for the grab bar, and off they went, whisked up or down the vertical belt to another floor. They passed through the hole in the ceiling or the floor, then stepped off on whatever level of the refinery they wished. The young women couldn't ride the man lift for apparent reasons but missed out on a unique experience.

Some young women began working at the TeaBag Station, whose product of small sugar packets could be found on every restaurant table in America. The Cube Station was a short distance away, where veteran women with good hand-to-eye coordination quickly and accurately grabbed a line of sugar cubes and packed them in precise rows in tiny boxes. Women looked up from their work in both locations, giving the young recruits a hardy wave. Their arrival was a novelty, and they couldn't help but wonder: Did everyone know about them and why they were working at the refinery? Indeed, the young women were a welcome diversion for the sisters.

~

In the summer of 1966, James Brown may have been right when he sang that the time was a man's world. This truism certainly existed at the refinery, where women were in the minority, and their tasks were relegated to gender-based duties such as clerical work, sewing, and packing sugar. The Equal Rights Amendment had yet to pass, and as of 2024, it has not yet been ratified by Congress. In 1966, women couldn't apply for a credit card independently, and most weren't searching for glass ceilings to break; women were trying to get their foot in the door, scanning for opportunities. However, C&H Sugar's extending temporary summer work to the daughters of employees was a game changer for many young women. This opportunity may have been a small victory, but it was significant. They had broken the sugar ceiling for their generation. Under the watchful eyes of the sisterhood in the locker room and with their support, Barbara and others like her paved the way for young women to work at the refinery that summer and for summers to come. For college-bound female recruits, employment at the refinery allowed them to earn enough money to pay for one year at a college or university. They stood on the sisters' shoulders so others could stand on theirs.

Chapter Eight
Packing War Sugar for Vietnam

"Shut it Down!" yelled D.J. at the top of his lungs over the refinery's din. Hearing his urgent command, his team packing ten-pound cloth bags of sugar to fulfill a government order headed for Southeast Asia responded immediately, quickly pulling levers and pushing buttons to shut the assembly line down. The metal chutes carrying free-flowing sugar and the conveyor belts carrying ten-pound bags promptly came to a noisy halt. The workspace became still and eerily quiet. A palpable fear swept over some of the new summer hires. Working at the refinery was a unique experience for them. Having heard stories from her father that powdered sugar occasionally ignited in the powder mill, Barbara was fearful, and that fear seemed to materialize today. However, the powder mill was in another part of the refinery complex, nearer to the warehouse than the main refinery. If this wasn't about the powder mill, what was it about? With her heart pounding and her muscles tensed, Barbara began to sweat, her mouth dry. Clammy and slightly light-headed, she wanted to run.

Barbara was new to the work environment since this was her first week at the refinery. She would have to adjust to the continuously loud noise level, the strange clattering mechanical sounds and groans, the dank, humid, heavy air, the smell of molasses, and the intense heat. Barbara looked around for cues from the old-timers, the veteran men and women who had worked at the refinery for decades. Did their faces show signs of fear? Their faces were expressionless, giving nothing away.

Barbara pulled herself together, and her anxiety began to subside. She didn't have to run for her life. Nothing had happened, at least not yet.

Not knowing if there was an emergency or a mechanical mishap, all remained quiet and focused, awaiting instructions. Most assumed those in charge would quickly identify and remedy the problem. Turning their attention to DJ, they noticed he showed no signs of stress. His customary broad smile was intact, his brilliantly white teeth standing out against his deep brown chestnut skin. With sheer delight, DJ sprang his robust, agile body like a hurdler to the top of wooden pallets laden with stacks of sugar bags, yelling, "And it's Boogaloo Time!" With this command, young men, summer help, who had started working at the refinery before the young women danced to imaginary music. The old-timers looked on and laughed at the commotion. This "crisis" seemed somehow routine to them. Barbara joined in, ever so tentatively and briefly. Her participation in the mayhem was conditional. It was as if she was cautiously sticking her toes in the deep end of a swimming pool before committing herself to diving in. Having recently broken the sugar ceiling, Barbara didn't want to jeopardize her new job; she wanted to show she was grateful and capable in her new position. Yet, she also wanted to show her willingness to be part of an already-established team tradition.

Because DJ was a permanent employee at the refinery, he had figured out what he could get away with. He had calculated that Jack, his competent, formidable foreman, had completed his morning rounds and was off checking on another of his production crews somewhere else in the vast ancient refinery. It was then that DJ dared set this scene in motion. Relaxed and a bit cheeky, he contrasted with Jack, who was always stiff, rigid, and on edge. Jack, a clipboard in his hands, was efficient and business-like, carefully setting himself apart from his production crews. In business casual attire, Jack wore a white short-sleeved shirt with a plastic pen liner containing several pens in his breast pocket, a necktie, black pants, black shoes with white socks, and a shiny white pristine plastic hard hat. Jack's necktie, a nod to his manager status, was probably a clip-on stored in his desk drawer overnight. It likely never left the refinery.

The prank lasted less than a minute, for the team didn't want to draw attention to itself lest someone think it wasn't being productive, not meeting quotas, or getting the job done. However, DJ repeated the horseplay whenever he sensed low energy or morale. He intuited when the team needed an infusion of tomfoolery to help relieve the monotony, repetitiveness, and tedium of refinery assembly line work. This simple, brilliant act provided the laughter and movement needed to blow off a little steam. The machines were turned on in a few minutes, and everyone returned to work.

DJ, the young leader of the team packing war sugar, was a lean, muscular man who always dressed in 501 Levi's, a white t-shirt, and a red and white cowboy bandana fashioned into a doo-rag that covered his hair. He worked in the Production Department at the refinery and kept things lighthearted. In his mid-thirties, DJ had no worries about the draft because of his age. Unlike most young Crockett summer hires who lived in a semi-rural, tight-knit, homogeneous, sheltered immigrant community, he lived in the Iron Triangle area of urban Richmond, California. He was street-smart and a natural-born leader who worked hard for his paycheck.

Working at the refinery with this diverse, motley crew packing war sugar for Vietnam demonstrated to the young women hires that growing up in Crockett had sheltered them from the broader world. Most were naïve and unprepared for college. Could they move away from Crockett, out of their comfort zone, and succeed at university?

The team worked in a temporary space on the refinery's fourth floor, just outside the women's locker room. As it was called in the plant, the government contract or order required ten-pound bulk sugar bags called cotton pockets to be packed for shipment to Vietnam. In late 1965, the U.S. Government substantially increased supply orders to C&H Sugar for the Vietnam War. The company had produced sugar during World War II.

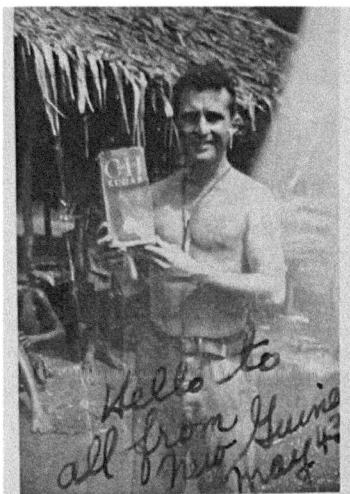

Faustino Pagni sent a photo home that was published in the Cubelet Press in 1943

Old friends *meet in New Guinea. Here Faustino Pagni (Cube Station) holds up a battered carton of C and H sugar that crossed the equator to provide food for American fighting men who are battling the Japs in the world's toughest theatre of war. In the background are some natives who seem to be wondering what all the shooting's about. Faustino has inscribed his best regards to all his many friends in Crockett.*

At the war's end, the refinery stored the equipment necessary for future use to meet the government's stringent quality and moisture control requirements. Once the order was completed, the team dispersed to other units in the Production Department throughout the refinery. Some young women eventually moved to the third floor to pack one-pound boxes of sugar cubes and sugar packets for restaurants. Others would pack one-pound boxes of granulated sugar, and some would be assigned to the powder mill.

Most recruits worked the dayshift, 8:00 a.m. to 4:30 p.m., and didn't have to adjust physically and mentally to a new shift schedule. That situation would come in a few weeks. The team of about ten workers was organized along gender lines. Women packed the sugar, sewed the bags, and swept the floor while the men did all the heavy lifting. Everyone rotated through their assigned tasks every thirty minutes, which helped relieve the boredom and monotony that seeped like a dense bay fog into every eight-hour shift, especially after lunch.

Since the team worked in a small space near the women's locker room, many employees, family, and friends walked past them during the day and waved at the young summer hires while they worked. Some stopped for a quick conversation. Many family members demonstrated pride in the fact that some young workers were the third generation of their family to work in the factory. This multi-generational loyalty was honored and respected by the company and the community. An article in the February 24, 1949, issue of the *Cubelet Press* noted that family tradition played an essential part in producing C&H Sugar's products. It listed 117 families where two or more generations worked at the refinery, detailing the family names, employee names, and relationships. A total of

278 employees, or about 14 percent of C&H Sugar's work-force, were represented in the article. The article also noted that familial loyalty contributed to creating a high-quality product and supported the company's ability to stay in business despite stiff market competition.

The workspace on the fourth floor was designed to pack ten-pound sugar bags. At the beginning of the assembly line, a large metal chute hung from the ceiling. It delivered exactly ten pounds of granulated cane sugar at precisely timed intervals.

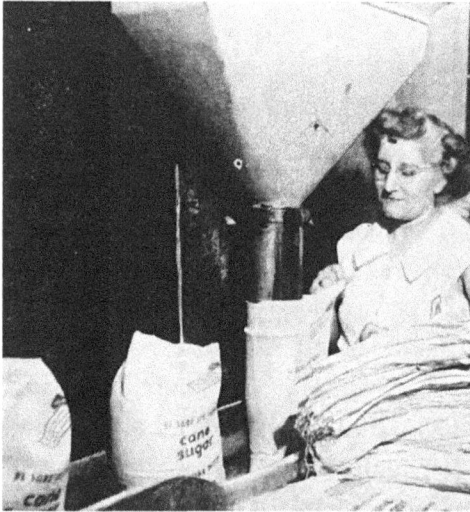

Louise Magnaghi catching granulated sugar in ten-pound cotton bags

Sugar dropping from the ceiling was like magic for the young women unfamiliar with the refinery. A woman stationed at the chute would pick up a bag from a large stack with her left hand, place it under it, and then catch the sugar in the bag as it dropped. Another woman would replenish the bags in the stack when necessary, so the process was continuous. The muslin cotton bags were silk-screened with the C&H Sugar logo, and a description of the contents was included in red and blue ink. The job's challenge was to hold the empty bag on the chute and anticipate when the sugar would fall from above. Holding the bag too loosely would result in the bag collapsing and sugar dumping on the conveyor belt, delivering a lapful of warm sugar to the woman sitting at the sewing machine. Holding the bag with the proper tension enabled the bag to fill correctly. With the sugar securely in the bag, the woman at the chute would steady it upright on the conveyor belt, carrying it to the next woman seated at an industrial sewing machine about six feet away.

The sewing machine was different from home machines. Its needle was horizontal, not vertical. The operator had to pull the upright sugar bag into the sewing machine and activate the needle with her knee pressed to a paddle. Then she pulled the top of the bag through the needle, guiding the material with her right hand's second and third fingers—this required concentration. The sewing machine operator had to position her fingers correctly with care for fear that the needle would sew across and through them. This never happened.

The sewing machine, threaded with heavy-duty cotton thread, created a chain stitch across the top of the bag, sealing the bag shut. Sometimes, the bags were sewn incorrectly and had to be reopened. Once opened, the bag was thrown away, and the sugar was collected, remelted, and refined again. Veteran workers knew how to pull out the sewed chain correctly, magically unraveling the stitches and opening the bag without effort. No knives or scissors were required.

Cutting the thread and steadying the bag on the belt was the last task before the bag traveled to the loading area, where young men grabbed it and threw it onto a wooden palette. The bag was then ready for shipment. When the palette was fully loaded, it was moved to the warehouse by a jitney, a hand-operated, battery-powered flat wagon. The warehouse crew prepared the palettes for shipment and loaded them onto train cars or trucks, ready for shipment overseas to Southeast Asia, typically through the Port of Oakland.

Sometimes, the sewing machine jammed due to a buildup of cotton filaments, the stitch tension went out of adjustment, or the thread had manufacturing defects and quickly broke. These issues resulted in poorly sewn bags whose top seams were weak and unable to withstand the stresses of packing and shipment. Fortunately, in-house expert mechanics were on hand to repair and adjust the machines, quickly responding to urgent calls from the sewing machine operator. Concerned with efficiency and not wanting to waste time, the mechanics often replaced a half-used spool with a new one.

Discarded spools usually had a lot of thread left on them. Some of these partial spools were used for other purposes in the factory. Others found their way into the women's locker room or employees' homes. As survivors of the Great Depression and World War II shortages, the women, immigrants, transplants, and first-generation Americans learned from their parents and their own experiences to save anything useful. Waste not, want not ruled the day, and many spools made their way home. Crockett's children used the string to fly kites. It was used around the house and for craft projects such as crocheting edges for pillowcases or dishtowels and making doilies and tablecloths. Some women made small projects like Christmas ornaments, while others made large projects like tablecloths and bedspreads. Veteran women worked on their projects during breaks and lunchtime in the locker room, where friends exchanged popular craft patterns and cake recipes alike.

If sugar spilled onto the wood floor, a woman was assigned to sweep it up. Working in thirty-minute intervals, it was swept up and dumped into large cardboard drums. Because little sugar fell on the floor, this job tended to be tedious. The sweeper had plenty of idle time while she waited for sugar to spill. Sometimes, the sweeper stood leaning on the broom handle, waiting for sugar to sweep, or she chatted with people walking by. While wishing to sit, she couldn't lest she be considered unnecessary and let go. For example, Barbara feared she would be laid off before she had saved enough money for college. Waiting for sugar to spill was like working on a road crew, waiting for a load of asphalt to arrive. A fresh spill would spring the sweeper to action. The push broom's brush was about two feet across, making it large and unwieldy, and the industrial dustpan was equally large and awkward to use. At the end of the day, the drums filled with spilled sugar were retrieved by a forklift driver, and the sugar, called remelt, was recycled and re-processed in the refinery.

Cool and comfortable when the day shift began at 8:00 a.m., by the end of the day, work areas in the refinery, with all its machinery operating and the heat of a Crockett summer day, became stifling hot, well over ninety degrees. Sweat ran down Barbara's back and legs. Sugar dust in the air added to her discomfort. As sugar was continuously dropped into bags on the conveyor belt throughout the day, the air filled with sugar dust. This delicate, sweet dust settled on everyone's hair and every exposed part of their bodies. One could taste it. The most troublesome area was the crook of the arm at the elbow. The stickiness could drive Barbara wild whenever she bent and straightened her arms. This discomfort became annoying, and Barbara had to work hard to control herself. The annoyance made her realize that working at the refinery required as much physical as well as mental effort. She needed better coping skills and resilience to go the distance or wash out. It was going to be a very long, hot summer!

When Barbara became bored or physically uncomfortable, she often watched the minutes tick by on the oversized industrial clock on the wall. Clock-watching became an obsession and a big mistake. Watching the hands of the clock move ever so slowly was like waiting for a pot of water to boil—tick, tick, tick. Barbara tried to look away from the clock and not look back, but she did—tick, tick, tick. Time seemed to be standing still or moving slowly—tick, tick, tick. Having always had something to keep her busy and distracted at school, this was a new experience for her. How would she redirect her attention from the clock to get through each day, week, month, and summer?

The veteran women mentored the young workers, watching, correcting, and teaching them to work efficiently with minimal effort. Sometimes, they suggested how they might stand or hold their hands in a specific way. The veteran workers led by example. Their work habits showed the young women to work diligently, consistently, and hard. They were loyal employees devoted to the refinery, its people, and each other. They were prompt and rarely missed a day of work. Evidence of this is the March 1978 issue of the

Cubelet Press, which noted that Louise Magnaghi had had perfect attendance for four years and six months in the refinery's Production Department. Louise's performance was typical of many refinery employees.

The veteran workers were survivors and taught the young women to be the same. Some sisters were unassuming and quiet and spoke up only when necessary, keeping their focus, opinions, and thoughts to themselves. Others spoke up and "didn't suffer fools," as they would say. The young women watched as these strong, dependable, unfailing workers pushed through the heat and discomfort. They dressed neatly; their hair coiffed beautifully. They wore costume jewelry and pretty hankies, accomplishing what was asked of them without fuss or stress. Some didn't appear to sweat and never complained. They were reliable and stable, never showing emotion, and they always wore a smile. Like the veterans, the young women learned to keep their thoughts to themselves, creating an inner world and dialogue that sustained them throughout the day. These habits were the coping mechanisms necessary for them to survive the summer.

The sisterhood in the locker room was most evident during breaks and the lunch period. Entering the locker room, everyone quickly washed the sugar dust and sweat from their faces, arms, and legs in a large, round stone handwashing sink. Then, women drank water or coffee to stay hydrated and awake. Once refreshed, all gathered in the dining area, where there was always something to eat. There were doughnuts at break time in the morning and extraordinary cakes to sample at lunch or the last break of the day. While eating, groups debriefed on what had happened during the shift or shared gossip about their team. While there were no laws or rules about sexual harassment in the work-place, the women had their methods for handling catcalls and unwanted attention from men. The veteran women quickly noted which men were too aggressive, flirtatious, players, as they called them, and the importance of staying away from them. There was plenty of unsolicited advice, but grateful, the young women listened intently and cherished the camaraderie.

After physically mastering the skills to do her job, it was essential for Barbara to develop emotional stamina. She passed the time by thinking about the sugar's destination, Vietnam. With all the newspaper and TV publicity about the war and so many of her friends leaving for Vietnam, the subject was ever-present in her mind and the minds of most young men and women. In 1966, controversy and conflict surrounding the Vietnam War divided the country, genera-tions, and to some degree, families. Many of the summer hires' parents had fought in World War II, some with im-pressive combat records. Crockett also had its share of those who had survived Pearl Harbor. Some fathers had fought in Salamaua, New Guinea, a prolonged continuous battle in the Pacific Theater, while others had fought in the Battle of the Bulge. A statue of St. Anthony at St. Rose of Lima Catholic Church was gifted by one of these men who prayed so fervently to St. Anthony while fighting at the Battle of the Bulge that he vowed to build a monument to the saint if he survived. Surviving, he fulfilled his promise. These local he-roes became members of the Veterans of Foreign Wars, reg-ularly attending meetings at the American Legion Hall on Pomona and Alexander Streets. They marched in Sugar City Festivals or rode on the poignant patriotic floats they made.

Many fathers had mixed emotions about whether the

United States should be fighting a war in Vietnam. They had a strong sense of duty to the United States but didn't want to see their sons go to war. Some kept these feelings to themselves, while others argued about the merits of the war. There were loud, heated arguments around the dinner table sparked by video clips families regularly watched on local and national news. Besides the videos showing horrific daily scenes of jungle combat, there were pictures of casualties and reports on the number of enemy and American soldiers killed or wounded. The war was being measured and quantified, and the statistics reported daily were sobering and heartbreaking. Television documented and convinced some of how costly the war was regarding lives and resources. Some sisters in the locker room mentioned that getting through World War II would have been impossible for them had they seen this vivid, visual information daily. Because of news blackouts and letter censorship during World War II, they never knew where their loved ones fought until they returned home.

The arguments against the merits of the war coincided with the young generation's questioning and often rejecting authority. Appalled by the devastation and violence, some opposed the war on moral grounds and became conscientious objectors. Others fled to Canada to avoid the draft and never returned, while some went to war and were wounded or killed. Friends went to war and returned home, never the same, while some came home intact and resumed their lives. There were so many unanswered questions. Why was the United States intervening in a foreign civil war when it had not been attacked? What were the objectives of the war? Was the war winnable? Did it have an end? Was the threat of Communism an existential threat to the United States?

Keeping its promise to inform its employees about the political climate in which C&H Sugar found itself, the January 1966 *Cubelet Press* reported that the North Vietnamese Communist government had received a gift of sugar from Cuba's Fidel Castro. Reprinted from the *San Francisco Examiner*, an article in the *Cubelet Press* stated that North Vietnam had received 10,000 tons of sugar from Cuba. It quoted a Cuban newspaper article, "The sugar was a modest contribution to the heroic fight of the Vietnamese people against Yankee Imperialism." The gift of sugar demonstrated Cuba's solidarity with the government and the people of Vietnam. The *Cubelet Press* also listed the names of refinery employees who went to war and noted that positions with the refinery would be held for those who wished to return to C&H Sugar after the war ended.

The November 1966 issue of the *Cubelet Press* reported that the C&H Sugar Softball Association was collecting discarded equipment for soldiers and children in South Vietnam. Sergeant Roger L. Karl formed softball teams among Vietnamese children, hoping that playing an organized sport with G.I.s would teach local children more about the Americans in their country. The program was not affiliated with the U.S. Army. Sergeant Karl also wished to give the G.I.s something fun to do in their off-hours.

Some of the young men, temporary workers at the plant, were college students with medical or student deferments. Unlike many young men in America, they had access to information and alternatives that allowed them to avoid being sent to Vietnam. Others joined the Army Reserves or National Guard to avoid the draft. Deferments weren't available to everyone, and many local young men who joined the military were shipped out to Southeast Asia soon after graduating from high school. The young men on the fourth floor talked about their hopes, fears, and plans to avoid Vietnam, but the politics of the war was never discussed. It would have been a flashpoint nobody wanted to ignite.

∼

By the end of summer, having worked various shifts with multiple teams on numerous types of jobs throughout the Production Department in the refinery and having experienced the sisterhood of the women's locker room and the support and encouragement that came with it, Barbara was determined and confident to move on to her new future.

Chapter Nine
Going the Distance

Long-distance runners train to endure the physical pain and mental distress of reaching the eighteenth mile of a twenty-six-mile marathon. The runner's vision of the finish line disappears in the distance, a mirage at the end of a hot, blurry, shimmering vision. Everything hurts, the physical pain is intense, and the body continually sends messages to the brain to stop running. The runner's mental and physical challenges are like working through the physical discomfort and mental distress associated with life's complicated, risky challenges of long durations, large or small. The second trimester of a high-risk pregnancy or the seventh hour of a fourteen-hour flight from San Francisco to Sydney, Australia, comes to mind. Wishing the pregnancy was in its final month or frequently checking the airplane's in-flight map are futile. The only way forward is to find a way to negotiate through such challenges, such as developing coping mechanisms and arriving at the end, the finish line, victorious and intact, mind, body, and spirit.

Once the novelty of being a new female summer hire at the plant wore off, Barbara found herself figuratively at the eighteenth mile of a twenty-six-mile marathon. Though elusive, the mental stamina to go on had to be found lest the finish line, saving enough money to go to college, wouldn't be reached. The first step was to accept and commit to working through what was sometimes an uncomfortably long hot summer and early fall, four months at the refinery.

The government order for the Vietnam War was completed,

and the teammates dispersed to new assignments throughout the refinery's Production Department. Most had enjoyed working on the government order, especially in the company of a team consisting primarily of college students. The teammates shared much in common and many laughs, but it was time to move on. Barbara worried there wouldn't be another leader like DJ to challenge her seriousness, help her laugh at herself, and show her how to let off steam. Others were concerned about learning new skills and working through a rotating series of ten-day work shifts–day, swing, and graveyard.

But move on, they did. Some moved to the production department's small pack section on the refinery's second floor. Small pack referred to the small products produced there, including teabags and sugar cubes. Teabags referred to tiny rectangular paper sugar packets containing a single serving of sugar.

Old teabags on display at the Crockett Historical Museum

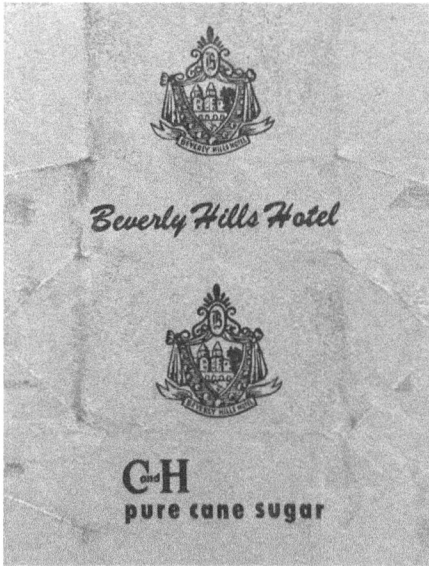

*An unfilled teabag designed
for the Beverly Hills Hotel*

The packets were in sugar bowls on most restaurant dining tables. The two names were used interchangeably in the plant. The sugar packets, preferred by restauranteurs to sugar bowls for neatness and sanitary reasons, were customized to advertise the logo and name of a restaurant or point of interest in the country. When New Yorker Benjamin Eisenstadt's cafeteria business declined in the mid-1940s, he used his teabag-making machinery to develop sugar packets, thus the name. In the mid-1950s, Mr. Eisenstadt founded Cumberland Packing and manufactured, marketed, and distributed Sweet' N Low, a saccharin sweetener.

A coping mechanism Barbara developed was playfully creating stories about her work environment. For example, Barbara imagined she was the missing piece of the large

177

packing machine that had yet to be fully automated. The machine, filled with bulk sugar and a massive roll of paper, folded and enclosed a small amount of sugar, likely a teaspoon, into a packet. At each machine, women packers were seated on adjustable, padded swivel chairs at the end of two long trays, one on each side. The women collected packets

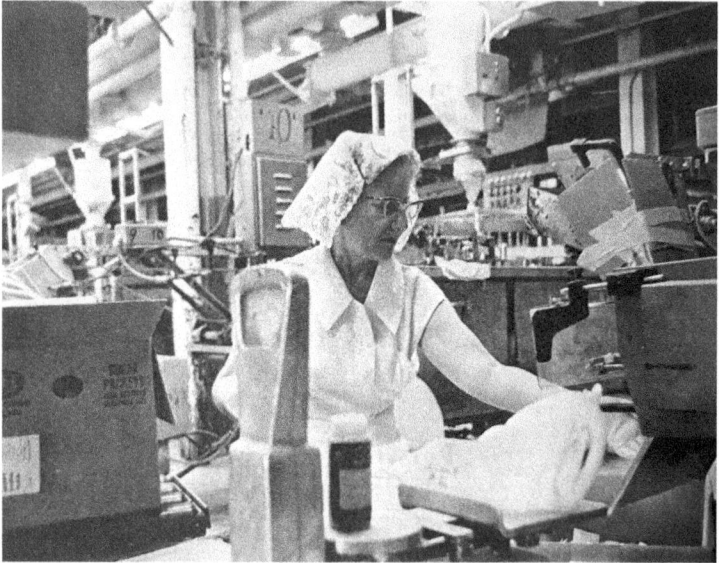

Louise Magnaghi working at the Teabags Station

that exited the machine into a small one-pound cardboard box. Quickly folding boxes designed with C&H Sugar's logo, the packer placed the box on a form, one on each side, at the end of each tray. She alternately pulled and scooped the sugar packets into the box using each hand's second and third fingers. Pressing her foot to an activator on the floor, a vibrator settled the sugar packets in the box. Once the box was filled, she placed it onto a conveyor belt that automatically gathered the correct number of boxes and packed them into a carton for shipment.

The challenge of this position was to create a relaxed rhythm so that the packer alternately filled one box on the right and one on the left. Overfilling or underfilling the box caused havoc. Occasionally, when a box was overfilled, the packer had to grab and remove a few packets, quickly throwing them to the floor to keep the line moving. Conversely, if the box was incomplete, the packer had to wait for more packets, and her rhythm was broken. When efficient, the packer could reach ahead and pull the correct number of packets early, resulting in a few extra seconds of idle time before the next box had to be filled. The mental games some of the young women played to pass the time!

A black registration mark at the top of the packet's long edge signaled that the paper was aligned correctly in the packing machine. The mark was on the right or the left, depending on which tray the packet exited the machine. If the mark was a quarter of an inch from the edge of the sugar packet, the printed message on the front and back of the packet was aligned correctly and could easily be read. The paper was misaligned if the black mark appeared elsewhere at the top, such as in the middle of the long edge. When the paper was misaligned, the packer shut the machine down and called a mechanic, who promptly adjusted and re-registered the paper roll. Once the mechanic restarted the machine, the production and packing process began anew. Sometimes, the mechanic couldn't adjust the paper perfectly on the first try, resulting in his starting and stopping the machine several times and throwing more improperly made packets to the floor. The woman assigned to floor-sweeping swept and emptied the discarded packets into a cardboard drum for remelting and reprocessing. All work areas had to be kept immaculately clean. The women rotated from machine to machine every thirty minutes, sweeping the floors and returning to the packing machines.

Working at the Teabags Station

New to the experience, Barbara felt trapped in place by the industrial process and wondered why the packing machine hadn't been completely automated. She created metaphors for how the packets advanced from the machine to pass the time and break her thoughts of feeling trapped and suited only for tedious, repetitive, and monotonous work. It was amusing to think of the sugar packets marching in lines two-by-two like a marching band or soldiers on parade. Other times, the packets danced in a long line like the New York City Rockettes. The pitfalls of repetitive work had returned for Barbara. Clock-watching started anew with a vengeance, and time dragged on—tick, tick, tick.

The second floor of the refinery was busy. A hub of social activity gathered around the man lift. Barbara enjoyed watching workers getting on or off and wondering how many floors they had traveled. It was mesmerizing to watch riders standing upright while traveling from floor to floor, up and down. It was as if they were traveling inside the pneumatic tubes once used in hospitals and department stores. Men or women in pants appeared, their heads or feet first. Then their whole body appeared and soon disappeared as if beamed off the Starship Enterprise. Men often stopped by and engaged the women in personal, one-on-one conversations. Barbara enjoyed most discussions, especially those about current events. To avoid talking to some men, Barbara signaled uncomfortably that she didn't want to speak by acting busy, glancing down or away, and avoiding eye contact. These evasive moves usually worked, but not always.

The young women observed how the veteran women worked. They learned to be more efficient. Intrigued, they observed how the veterans dressed and interacted with others. Most women dressed with pride and confidence. Every woman in production wore a pristine white uniform, washed, bleached, starched, and ironed to perfection. Some women wore pretty color-coordinated hankies in their pockets, makeup, and costume jewelry, including earrings with matching necklaces. Hairstyles were typical of the big hairstyles of the sixties when hair was back-combed and teased high to create volume, then brushed smooth and sprayed into shape. Rita's hairstyle, called a beehive, was particularly fascinating. Rita's long hair had been teased, gathered, and wrapped, then secured neatly at the back of her head with hairpins and a substantial amount of hair spray. Not wanting sugar dust to collect in her hair, Rita used two hairpins to pin a colorful square cotton hanky to the top of her head each day. As the days passed, and more sugar dust landed on Rita's hair, her hair changed color, becoming lighter by the day. By the end of the ten-day shift, Rita's hair had changed from dark brown to tan and was probably stiff as a board.

The physical environment at the teabag station was similar to what the young women had already experienced on the fourth floor. Sugar dust was ever-present. Barbara developed dermatitis on her face, which calmed as she learned to take every opportunity to wash her face. The giant rolls of paper and the granulated sugar heated up inside the massive packing machines, and that aroma, mixed with molasses, made for another fascinating scent. Barbara noticed this new aroma in the morning when she arrived at her machine, but her sense of smell gradually faded, and by day's end, she could no longer detect it.

All the young summer hires were given an audition at the cube station to determine if they had the hand-to-eye coordination required to pack sugar cubes. With the foreman, Jack, at their side, veteran sugar cube packers demonstrated how to fit the cubes into tiny boxes. The young women watched the veterans work quickly, effortlessly, and efficiently. They made the job look easy, and the new hires felt confident they could do it, as well as the veterans. The tiny sugar cubes advanced along a tray towards a steel form, where a veteran assembled the correct number of sugar cubes before placing them in the box. The challenge for the packer was to grab the exact amount of cubes and move them to the form in mid-air. Gripping and moving the cubes with the correct pressure was the elusive trick the young women had to master. Applying too much pressure sent the

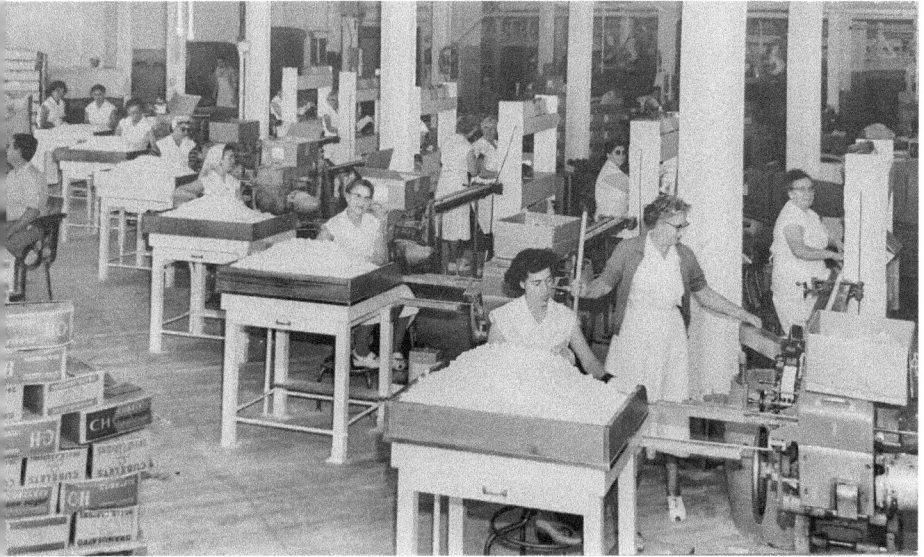

Working at the Cube Station

cubes arching into the air, spilling onto the floor. Applying insufficient pressure resulted in the cubes arcing down and falling. The sugar cubes that fell to the floor were remelted and reprocessed. After a half-hour demonstration, the young women were invited to try, but the job proved much more challenging than it looked. None of the young women could master the required techniques and failed their cube station auditions.

Large industrial fans circulated the air in the packing areas on hot, sweltering days. Visiting the long, expansive wooden docks located on the Carquinez Strait from the old refinery to the warehouse to cool off was discouraged. Safety was the paramount concern. Nevertheless, an old timer such as a relative could be convinced to take a new hire to the waterfront to cool off at lunchtime. Located on

183

the straits, one could experience the water lapping against the docks, how the water smelled, and, most importantly, how the water cooled the air. The contrast of the fresh, cool air washing over one's skin or damp, sweaty uniform was shocking and brought pleasant chills. For the young recruits who had grown up in Crockett, the sights and smells on the waterfront brought back childhood memories of fishing on the straits, visits to Dowrelio's or the Bass Club, or the Garden City Ferry on a hot summer day.

Once the dayshift and four shutdown days were over, some young women worked at the teabags station on the swing shift, 4:00 p.m. to 12:00 a.m. They reported to work on a Wednesday and worked the next ten days straight until the shift was over the following Friday. Working the swing shift was enjoyable because it allowed the young women free time to be active during the day. Their high school or neighborhood friends worked, so they couldn't spend time with them swimming at the new swimming pool at Alexander Park, for example. After a pleasant day, one could leave for work at about 3:15 p.m., work a shift, and return home by about 12:20 a.m. The trick was to get to bed at a reasonable hour to wake up and enjoy the following day before another night of work. Barbara developed an interesting coping mechanism. She pretended she was going to a party that started every day at 4:00 p.m. This technique worked well and kept her happy.

The refinery was beautifully illuminated at night. The iconic flashing, colorful C&H Sugar sign made the refinery building sparkle outside, while the interior lighting, though antiquated in some areas, provided a pleasant glow. The cool sea breezes and the summer fog that crept into the Carquinez Straits at night shrouded the refinery, enveloping it and cooling its century-old bricks. As a result, the refinery was more comfortable at night than during the day shift when heat seemed to build much like a slowly developing crescendo until it reached a blasting fortissimo.

After working ten days on the swing shift and enjoying four days off, some young women were assigned to the graveyard shift from 12:00 a.m. to 8:00 a.m. The graveyard shift meant they would have to develop even more effective coping mechanisms. This was difficult for Barbara. Her body couldn't adjust to sleeping during the day and working the night, and she never recovered over the ten-day work schedule. Having no energy, she was constantly tired and sleepy and felt she could sleep standing up. This was especially challenging when sweeping the floors and picking up packets. Barbara was in a daze, a muddle. Mamie and Louise, sisters from the locker room who were friends and mentors, noticed Barbara was struggling, and they went into action, teaching her the skills needed to get through the graveyard shift. They were veterans of decades of shift work and knew how to cope. Mamie suggested Barbara have lunch during her first break at 2:00 a.m. Eating her lunch early allowed Barbara to sleep during her lunch break, 4:00 to 4:25 a.m.

A sofa covered in Naugahyde fabric served as her bed, and her blankets were the day's numerous leftover newspapers strewn in piles throughout the locker room. Stretching out on the sofa, Barbara covered herself with several layers of newspapers. It was easy to imagine herself as a character in Jack Kerouac's novel, *On the Road,* or a transient sleeping on a park bench or in the rail cars passing by the refinery. The plastic upholstery made Barbara sweat, but she didn't care–she was comfortable enough. Louise woke Barbara at

4:25 a.m. so she could get up and rewash her face. She wet the front of her uniform to stay cool. After all this preparation, Barbara returned to the large packing machines, which started promptly at 4:30 a.m. At the 6:00 a.m. break, she ate fresh cinnamon toast and drank coffee prepared by Mamie or Louise. Finally energized with a snack, sugar, and caffeine, the long night was almost over by that hour, and the last two hours of the shift were manageable. The trick was to get home early, shower quickly, and fall asleep for a full day's slumber until the process repeated that night and for nine more.

The graveyard shift was equally challenging mentally. Barbara, fearing she wouldn't have enough energy to get through the night, didn't do much during the day except sleep, eat, relax, and nap while watching television. Sadness overcame her as she prepared to leave for work and watched her family retire to their comfortable beds for the night. After ten days, Barbara completed a full rotation through the shifts and returned to the dayshift. This felt good. Her perspective returned, and she pledged to persevere until the next graveyard shift a month later.

Receiving their paychecks every two weeks and watching their checking accounts grow kept the young women grounded and focused. Their salary rewarded them for working hard, pushing through the discomfort of the graveyard shift, and living outside their comfort zone. The young women joined the Sugar Workers Union Local #1 as a condition of their employment, and union dues were deducted from every paycheck. Some resented paying the dues because they were saving almost everything for college. They didn't understand that the dues were necessary to fund the union and its benefits, including past wage negotiations, security, healthcare, benefits, and all the hard work and sacrifices made by former union members. They were standing on the shoulders of past sugar workers and union organizers.

During the years after the catastrophic depression that followed the Stock Market collapse of 1929, C&H Sugar struggled to survive. Sugar prices fell. Under the leadership of George Morrison Rolph, the refinery's managers reduced employee positions, working hours, and wages to keep the refinery operating. During these challenging times, liberal labor laws enabled employees to organize to improve their rights and benefits. The Congress of Industrial Organizations (CIO), Sugar Workers Union, and the International Longshore and Warehouse Union (ILWU) struck in 1935 and 1937. In 1938, a bitter strike over which union had jurisdiction at the refinery tore the community of Crockett apart, pitting neighbors and family members against one another. The refinery closed. On March 16, 1938, over 600 women, wives of employees, met at the Crockett Community Auditorium. They passed a resolution petitioning C&H Sugar to honor the American Federation of Labor's (AFL) request to reopen the refinery. These local women wanted C&H Sugar's management and the unions to know the conflict had to end; their families were suffering. However, the CIO warehouse workers' union refused to settle their wage dispute with C&H Sugar, and the picket line remained. The refinery remained closed. Fighting began on the twenty-seventh day of the strike. Four hundred members of the AFL charged the CIO picket line, severely beating warehousemen and sugar workers. The CIO fought back, but the AFL drove the CIO workers from the refinery. Law enforcement agencies blocked all access to Crockett, including roads and rail lines, to ease tensions and prevent union reinforcements from entering Crockett. The bloody violence in the streets shocked residents and workers. In time, calm returned. The AFL gained control, and the refinery reopened. The CIO warehouse workers voted to accept the contract and return to work. In 1955, the AFL and CIO merged, ending their rivalry.

The young summer hires were packing for college. The swing shift was over; some were on the graveyard shift again. Barbara, the daughter of a veteran employee, was assigned to the powder mill with two veteran women. Working at the powder mill was a concern for Barbara because her dad had told her stories about how powdered sugar had ignited in the past.

Packing sugar in the Powder Mill

CHAPTER 9

Working at the powder mill was indeed different. With far fewer female employees, the women's locker room was a much smaller version of the main locker room on the fourth floor, and it lacked all its activity. An interior space without windows, it was dark and cramped. Notwithstanding the usual physical and mental graveyard struggles, the shift went on without a hitch until the last night, the eve of the 1967 Labor Day holiday. Working on this particular weekend had its advantages. First, the refinery windows provided a great view of all the pleasure boats heading east to the San Joaquin Delta from the San Francisco Bay through the Carquinez Straits. There was more pleasure boat traffic in those days, and as it was a holiday, boats flew festive flags from their rigging. It was like watching a boat parade. The second advantage was that workers earned a premium hourly wage for working the holiday–double time and a half. They received a significant bonus of two and a half times their regular hourly salary each hour!

The evening began as usual but at 12:45 a.m. Barbara felt the floor rise slightly and settle back down. All the machinery immediately shut down. Something had happened. Mechanics scurried about assessing the situation while the women chatted and awaited instructions. Moments later, the chief mechanic said, "OK, ladies. We've had a minor event that will take a little time to fix. You can head for the locker room, and I'll tell you when we are ready for you to return to work. Enjoy your rest." The mechanic had no idea how long it would take to fix the problem. Powdered sugar was brought to the powder mill by large screws, or worm drives, that directed the sugar far from the main refinery to the powder mill located over the warehouse. That evening

189

a small piece of metal broke off one of the screws, causing a spark that ignited the fine powdered sugar dust.

The women retired to the powder mill's locker room. Barbara quickly found a sofa, covered herself with newspapers, and readied for a short nap. Perpetually exhausted on this shift, she quickly relaxed and fell asleep. Six hours later, a mechanic knocked on the door to tell the women the machinery had been repaired and they could begin packing powdered sugar again. The machines started and quickly shut down, as the repair didn't hold. The women were done for the night, and the shift was over!

It was difficult for Barbara to hide her feelings. The graveyard shift was over for the summer, and a holiday weekend added to her delight. She had managed to sleep most of the night and was rested. Best of all, she had earned two and one-half times her usual hourly wage while sleeping and facing her fear.

As their tenure at the refinery ended and their move to university approached, many young women gathered in the locker room to look back over their summer. They talked about what they had learned from the working women, the sisters, at the refinery. From time spent together sharing experiences, stories, counsel, and examples, they recognized that these women embodied, demonstrated, and offered them friendship and sisterhood. The camaraderie these women provided was a precious gift, and the memory of their time together still is for most. The veteran women were an inspiration and a great example of what can be achieved when working together. The veterans had worked through and survived the Great Depression and World War II, often when their husbands and loved ones were away at war, and they had done so together. Events and challenges around them tested their friendships in the refinery and their community. Still, their relationships had endured for decades.

The working women also demonstrated that while living a simple outer life, they concealed a deeper private world each had created for themselves. They taught the young women to develop their secret inner worlds and coping mechanisms to survive the long, tedious, uneventful nights on the assembly line. No iPhones loaded with playlists or podcasts got them through the night. The women carried on in their inner worlds but outwardly shared their strengths, honesty, attitudes, loyalty, encouragement, tenacity, and laughter. Their memories continue to teach even to this day.

Perhaps the most significant gift the sisters gave the young women was acceptance. The veteran women accepted being born at a time and in a place that offered them limited opportunities. Lamenting that they would rather have had the chance to go to college, they accepted their reality while pushing the young women to achieve what they never could. They encouraged the young women to fight for their openings and their breaks. The veterans acknowledged and hoped the young women would build on the foundations that other women like them, whether immigrants, first-generation immigrants, transplants, or others, had made.

~

Leaving the refinery for the last time, Barbara began to understand that the lessons taught by these strong veteran women, the sisters, would serve her well as she embarked on her university adventure. She left the refinery humbled and grateful for working with and knowing them!

Chapter Ten

A New Reality

After spending several years discovering, reflecting upon, and researching the significance of my Aunty Lou's recipe collection and another four years actively writing this book, I believe I can identify for myself and perhaps others the factors that contributed to making life in Crockett so special. Recipients of C&H Sugar's progressive industrial relations policies and benevolence, *Benessere*, the small company-town environment with its amenities and unique culture, was for my generation and those generations that preceded mine Crockett's Golden Age.

Above all, Crockett's history is a microcosm of the history of the United States. Its history mirrors events throughout the country, including the arrival of European colonists who encountered and displaced indigenous people, the settling of the region through Mexican land grants, and the arrival of European immigrants and settlers. The California Gold Rush differentiated California by bringing a tsunami of people from throughout the world, resulting in California's rich cultural diversity and entrepreneurial spirit, which still exist today.

Due to Crockett's developing industries and geographic isolation and remoteness, immigrants and migrants arrived to find abundant employment opportunities but a lack of housing and amenities. C&H Sugar created an aggressive program to house workers and immigrants. In time, transplants found inexpensive land to build new homes. Italians, the largest immigrant group, re-created what many had left behind in Italy. Uprooted by immigration, neighbors sought security and comfort. They bonded with each other because of their commonalities and shared experiences, and a cohesive community developed and grew. Most residents were shielded from discrimination because those around them were just like them. Relationships and bonds among residents were deep, no matter their ethnicity.

The Italian culture in Valona was so pervasive that for immigrant and first-generation children, growing up in Valona was the same as growing up in Italy. In addition, it meant living in a bi-cultural environment–simultaneously experiencing 1950s progressive California and the early 1900s traditions and values brought over by their grandparents and parents. Children were often raised with strict values and practices that hadn't evolved in Crockett as in Italy.

Crockett's isolation, remoteness, and abundance of well-paying jobs led to its development as a walkable community. Crockett was self-sufficient and offered everything residents needed to thrive and prosper—a simple life full of opportunity, activities, and entertainment. Small businesses provided all the services a household could need. However, a fatal blow hit Crockett's small businesses in the mid-1950s. One hundred and fifty homes on Valona's west side were destroyed to build Highway 80 and the second bridge across the Carquinez Straits, reducing Crockett's population from about 5,000 to 3,300. Crockett was no longer isolated, and employees began to commute to the refinery from surrounding communities.

In the 1960s, C&H Sugar no longer needed to nurture a local workforce. Simultaneously, improvements and automation came to the refinery, and the company cut its workforce dramatically to remain competitive and profitable.

For example, in the 1920s and 1930s, a crew of about 300 men was needed to unload 5,000 tons of raw sugar in four days. By 1976, thanks to automation, two men on three eight-hour shifts, or one day's worth, could unload 23,000 tons of raw sugar. C&H Sugar amended its benevolent and paternalistic culture and reversed its intense community involvement strategy. Crockett ceased to be a quintessential company town.

Initially, Crockett floundered, being ill-equipped to manage its new independence. Unincorporated and accustomed to the paternalistic benevolence that had been the cornerstone of C&H Sugar's plan to recruit and retain its workforce, Crockett lacked a civic structure to respond quickly to the losses. Gift-giving to local children and the spectacular Christmas pageant came to an end. The beautifully maintained parks and numerous paths throughout town, once maintained by C&H Sugar's twenty-two gardeners, were neglected and became unkempt and abandoned. The Crockett Club, which housed the swimming pool and recreational facilities, was abandoned and demolished. All seemed lost, but the seeds of volunteerism and civic involvement sown in the hearts and minds of immigrant families years before in the Americanization classes held at the high school and those planted at the dedication of the Community Auditorium in 1920 began to germinate and grow.

With an initial investment from C&H Sugar and a sustaining three-year financial commitment, volunteers experienced in construction and community development led the effort to build a community pool in Alexander Park. The swimming pool at the Crockett Club was so popular that Crockett's residents felt they could not be without one. Today, the Crockett Recreation Department manages and maintains the swimming pool and offers various recreational programs for children and adults.

In 1971, the Crockett Improvement Association, CIA, was formed to address citizen well-being, including town beautification and cleanup. Since Crockett was and still is an unincorporated town of Contra Costa County, the CIA also became the liaison to the county. The CIA also began to tackle community issues such as policing, vandalism, and drugs. The relationship with Contra Costa County was never more critical than when the management of C&H Sugar decided it would no longer own the Community Auditorium. Fortunately, a volunteer Citizens Advisory Committee was created; its members responded by working with C&H Sugar and the County to save the Auditorium from demolition. The group also raised funds for much-needed renovations. Today, the Auditorium is autonomous and self-sufficient, managed by the Crockett Recreation Department. The activities at the Auditorium continue to focus on local community activities and events, just as Crockett's founders had hoped. Once an essential part of Crockett culture, community celebrations diminished over the years. However, the Sugar City Festival and the parade endured for many years and still exist in a modified format.

Community activism is alive and well in Crockett. The Crockett Historical Society was created in the late 1970s by Crockett volunteers who were interested in preserving the town's history. It was incorporated the same year as Crockett's 100th anniversary. The Museum opened its doors in September 1981 after volunteers cleaned, repaired, and painted the old Southern Pacific Railway Depot donated to the town by C&H Sugar. Crockett's first settler home, the Old Homestead, is still owned by C&H Sugar but is managed by the Carquinez Women's Club. The money earned from event rentals funds local student scholarships, community efforts, and events. In addition, the Crockett Chamber of Commerce's mission is "to model, advance, preserve business vitality, growth, and prosperity in Crockett and its neighboring communities." Though there are fewer social clubs, many are still thriving.

Perhaps the most obvious example of the new relationship between C&H Sugar and Crockett came in the mid-1980s with the announcement that C&H Sugar had contracted with Pacific Thermonetics of Texas and Menlo Park to build a 240-megawatt cogeneration power plant at the refinery. The proposed cogeneration power plant was to burn natural gas to supply steam and electricity to the refinery, reducing the refinery's annual energy costs. Pacific Thermonetics planned to sell the bulk of the energy produced to Pacific Gas and Electric Company over thirty years. While there was no public objection to a cogeneration power plant creating energy from C&H Sugar's steam, thus cutting the refinery's energy costs, there was opposition to the plant's size and what seemed to be a total disregard for the community's needs. Pacific Thermonetics proposed to build the power plant at the corner of Bay Street and Loring Avenue on C&H Sugar's property adjacent to the raw sugar storage bins. The site was directly across the street from the Loring Avenue residential area.

Four local young men, an architect, an attorney, an engineer, and a scientist named the Four Horsemen to the Apocalypse by those who favored building the plant, worked with local volunteers to create a committee called The Plant Busters. During community planning meetings, Crockett citizens suggested the cogeneration power plant be reduced in size and sited more appropriately on the other side of the sugar bins. This would protect residents from intrusive industry and noise. The community also requested environmental mitigations. If the plant had been sited as proposed, it would have obscured the views of this scenic waterfront neighborhood, the residential area would have been gravely affected, and property values on the east side of town would have plummeted. Pacific Thermonetics refused to modify its plans, and Crockett volunteers again rose to the occasion.

The proposed cogeneration power plant ignited discord among and within Crockett families, similar to the 1938 labor strike. There were conflicts between the generations living in town. Many older residents still working at the refinery couldn't imagine that C&H Sugar would propose anything harmful to the community. Many immigrants still saw C&H Sugar as their benevolent employer. They remembered the old company and its generous industrial relations policy—what it had done for them, their immigrant families, and the community. The younger generation fighting the proposal, many new to Crockett, didn't share these sentiments. They saw the relationship between C&H Sugar and the community not as benevolent but as paternalistic. Others were the children of long-time residents who had been recipients of C&H Sugar's benevolence. Several unions wanted the construction jobs the new plant would provide. A long, loud, protracted debate ensued, not in the streets but in homes, public opinion, newspaper articles, town hall meetings, and public meetings of the Public Utilities Commission, the Contra Costa County Board Supervisors, and the California Energy Commission in Sacramento.

Offering to work with Pacific Thermonetics to re-site, re-engineer, and mitigate safety and environmental concerns, the Crockett volunteers prevailed. The California Energy Commission rejected the original proposal because of the impact on Crockett, its lack of environmental mitigations, and Pacific Thermonetic's failure to sign the plant's proposal under penalty of perjury. Approximately two years later, another energy company proposed a new design for the co-generation plant and shared its willingness to work with the community. Not only was the proposed plant sited appropriately, but it also offered several improvements and mitigations to the community and its citizens.

Two persistent and capable women from Crockett volunteered and negotiated for six months with all parties to mitigate the plant's impacts. The power plant was reconfigured to lessen its visual impact. The sugar bins were painted, acoustical material was placed between each bin to diminish the noise transmitted to the residential neighborhood, and a $30 million compensation package was to be paid over thirty years to the community. As a result, the Crockett Community Foundation was created.

The Foundation's mission "is to enhance the quality of life in the Community, now and for generations to come." It is the best example of Crockett's volunteers' strength, tenacity, and commitment. The Foundation's goals are to serve the community, foster volunteerism, Crockett's fundamental value, and promote a sense of community. The Foundation is managed by a locally elected Board of Directors responsible to the community. It has established a permanent endowment to fund and support its future activities.

Crockett has evolved from an isolated, self-sufficient town to a suburb, a bedroom community, a tiny speck in the San Francisco Bay Area megalopolis. Easily accessible to most of the Bay region, it is uniquely located between San Francisco and Napa Valley. The COVID-19 pandemic has heightened interest in Crockett's moderately priced homes, with many transitioning to working from home. Homes have sold briskly to young families that would otherwise have been priced out of the region. Young parents with small children can be seen strolling in the neighborhoods—a good sign for the future. Small businesses are starting to return.

At a book reading in Benicia in the mid-1990s, I met Francis Mayes, author of *Under the Tuscan Sun*. Ms. Mayes was on a tour to promote her book, which became a best seller and a movie. The book recounted her life in Cortona, Italy, where she and her husband, Ed, remodeled an old villa and developed strong attachments with the community's citizens. Ed and I chatted about their lives in Italy, and he suggested I join them to enjoy their lifestyle, which was infused with Italian culture and strong relationships with neighbors. I responded in gratitude but told him I didn't need to travel to Italy; I already lived that lifestyle in Crockett. Our family still made wine, sausages, and ravioli, especially in the fall and Christmas. We also picked olives from the numerous olive trees growing in the steep hills of Valona, curing them in brine or lye. Friends still foraged for dandelion and wild mustard greens on these same hills in the spring, and several friends still hunted mushrooms. After researching and writing this book, I truly appreciate how much life in Crockett resembled that of Italy.

Someone once suggested that we live a portion of our lives in the past and part of our lives in the future, with the present being the most challenging. As my parents and Aunty Lou aged, they spent most of their days thinking about the past. My father daydreamed about his family, the culture he had left behind in Italy, and what life was like in Crockett and Valona "in the good old days." When Aunty Lou read her cake recipes, she reminisced and returned to the refinery, the sisterhood, and her friends in the Women's Locker Room.

Writing this book has helped me accept and reconcile that Valona's village way of life and my unique childhood are gone forever. However, the values, hopes, and inspiration left by our ancestors and forebears remain vibrant and embedded in Crockett's culture and our memories. From George Morrison Rolph to the beleaguered immigrants he and C&H Sugar helped, our predecessors were strong physically and emotionally. They had a vision for themselves and their community. They were risk-takers and worked hard for the welfare of their families, neighborhood, town, refinery, and Crockett generations to come.

~

The C&H Sugar Company, the immigrants, and the hardworking women at the refinery and its sisterhood are among Crockett's significant forebears, and their memory is beautifully embroidered in its history. Their contributions, sisterhood, and cake recipes are tangible artifacts of their legacy. For Crockett and Valona, an exquisite golden thread connects the past's stories to those of the present. Hopefully, this book and these stories bring to life the history and tales of Crockett and Valona and will inspire and enrich future generations.

Part 3

Cake Recipes
From the Locker Room

Chapter Eleven

Researching and Testing the Recipe Collection

A review of the cake recipes shared by the women in C&H Sugar's Women's Locker Room sparked a deeper examination of whether they would reveal their uniqueness to Crockett and the refinery. Three key questions emerged. First, could a chronological recipe timeline, informed by how the recipes were documented, ingredients used, and baking techniques, lead to a richer understanding of these recipes? Second, after testing the recipes in a home kitchen, would they require modification and adjustments for today's home bakers? And third, how were these cake recipes, a part of their shared heritage, disseminated throughout the community?

Chronological Recipe Timeline:

Organizing the recipes chronologically yielded two time categories: Early Cakes and Mid-Century Cakes. The Early Cakes, whose recipes date from 1939 to 1957, were handwritten or typed. They are one or two-bowl cakes made without an electric mixer from scratch. Some could be called dump cakes, as their ingredients are dumped into a bowl, stirred by hand, poured into a pan, and baked. Others could be called quick breads, as they are hearty, dense cakes baked in a loaf pan. Examples of Early Cakes include the Filled Cake Manele, Ciambella, Cinnamon Supper Cake, and the Gugelhumpf. In contrast, quick breads include the Squash Cake and the Wine Cake.

Mid-Century Cakes date from about 1957 to 1984 and were either mimeographed or photocopied. Some, but not all, are convenience cakes that use time and effort-saving short-cuts and processed ingredients, such as cake or pudding mixes. Large food manufacturers such as Betty Crocker and Duncan Hines developed and introduced modern lab-engineered cake and pudding mixes from the 1920s. Called quick mixes, Betty Crocker cake mixes became popular by 1947, and other food manufacturers joined in developing them further in the 1950s. Mid-Century Cakes include the Chocolate Sour Cream Kahlua Cake, Harvey Wallbanger Bundt Cake, and the Chocolate Cherry Bundt Cake.

Ms. Lynn Oliver, a former Midwestern reference librarian, investigated and compiled a history of food and has been called a food anthropologist or historian. Her *Food Timeline,* established online in 1999, was a helpful resource. as she investigated and compiled a history of food. After Ms. Oliver died in 2021, the Virginia Tech Special Collection and University Archives integrated Ms. Oliver's work and cookbook collections into a website, www.foodtimeline.org. Information from this source has been included with the cake recipes.

Testing:

Each cake was tested in a home kitchen using a consistent process and readily available ingredients. First, each recipe was carefully studied and baked following the original recipe. Once tested, the recipe was documented using a standard, consistent format. The original recipe was modified for current usage and accuracy when necessary. For convenience, ingredients were re-written in the order used.

When an error was discovered, a comparable recipe found in baking books or online was used to compare with the original. Necessary revisions were made, and the cake was rebaked until a successful cake was achieved. After baking and tasting each cake, baking notes and suggestions were added to the recipe.

For example, the Wine Cake originally listed one tablespoon of nutmeg, which seemed excessive. Nevertheless, the cake was baked, yielding a cake with a terrible metallic aftertaste. After examining the amount of nutmeg listed in similar recipes, the cake was baked again using only one teaspoon. The resulting cake was delicious, and the original recipe was revised. While mixing the ingredients for the Ciambella cake, the batter was far too dry, but nevertheless, the cake was baked. The resulting cake was so hard it could be rolled across the kitchen floor. After comparing other Ciambella recipes and more testing, the error was resolved by adding a half cup of milk.

Many women from the locker room emerged as skilled cake and dessert bakers. They used readily available ingredients for their baking, ingredients which differ in quality and taste today. Margarine or solid vegetable shortening, such as Crisco, was used instead of butter for the recipe's fat. If butter was used, it was salted. Today, unsalted butter is available, enabling the home baker to control the amount of salt in a recipe, which is critical for those on a salt-restricted diet. Unsalted butter also affects the taste of the finished cake, imparting a creamier, sweeter flavor than salted butter. Comparing the nutritional values of salted and unsalted butter, the only difference between the two is ninety grams of sodium. The recipes in this book were baked using unsalted butter, and the amount of salt was adjusted.

Some of the vintage recipes listed specific brand-name products. Assuming companies employed this practice to introduce or market their new products, brand names were changed to generic ingredients. For example, Swans Down flour or Sperry Drifted Snow flour became cake flour; Wesson Oil became vegetable oil, and a Betty Crocker Famous Honey Spice Cake Mix became a spice cake mix. Most of the recipes called for C&H Pure Cane Sugar. Still, following the chosen framework, generic names for sugar, such as granulated or powdered sugar, were substituted. However, pure cane sugar was used to test all the recipes. Waxed paper and brown paper bags were suggested to line cake pans. These were changed to baker's parchment paper, which is readily available today.

The size of cake pans, called cake tins in some recipes, was changed. Many recipes suggest baking the cakes in nine-inch pans. Still, many of these mid-century cakes were large in diameter and short in height. As a result, the pan size was changed to mirror today's aesthetic of smaller, taller cakes. Reducing the pan size to eight inches gave the desired effect; the finished cakes resembled what can be found in modern bakeries today.

The baking equipment for most vintage recipes was simple: a bowl, spoon, and a pan. Vintage kitchens were also equipped with a wire whisk, an old-fashioned, hand-cranked egg beater, wooden spoons, and bowls. Electric mixers, such as a General Electric MixMaster, were introduced later. A Kitchenaid food mixer was used to test these recipes. Some modern recipes need specific pan types for a successful bake, and these are noted in the recipes.

The first time the Harvey Wallbanger cake was tested, it didn't rise high enough. Ingredients were checked, and no

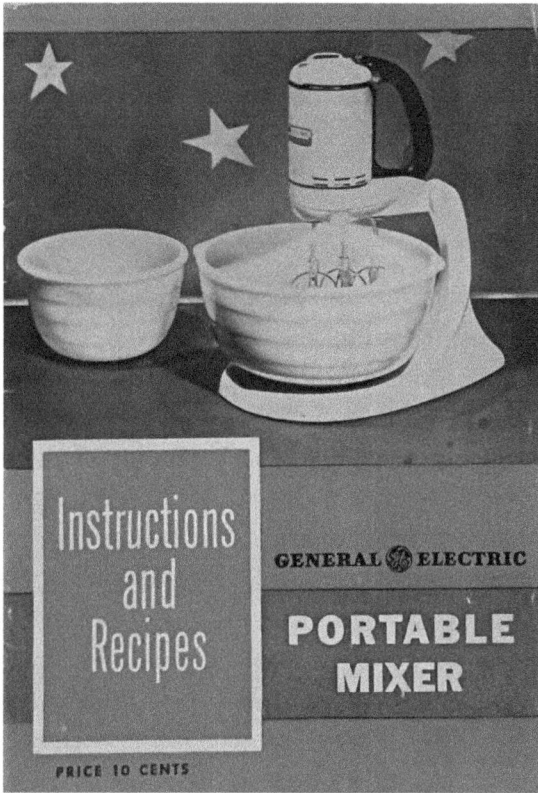

The owner's manual for an early electric mixer

errors were found; however, an internet search revealed that today's cake mixes weigh 15.25 ounces, compared to the 18.25 ounces they weighed about five years ago. An unexpected discovery! This weight change was significant enough to affect the outcome of the collection's old recipes. It would also affect recipes inherited, passed down from families and friends, or found in community cookbooks. A collapsed cake could cause a baker to question their ability to bake or wonder if grandma or auntie had left out a key ingredient.

Not so! Over the past few years, as food companies maintained the price of their cake mixes, the box size stayed the same, but the amount of product in the box was reduced. Perhaps food manufacturers thought the weight change would be less noticeable than a price increase. However, the deception can produce a less-than-satisfying or failed bake when using a vintage recipe.

To increase the amount of cake mix, bakers can buy another cake mix to add the additional three ounces of mix or use what *Better Homes & Gardens* calls a Cake Mix-Upizer. The upsizer mixes 1-1/2 cups of all-purpose flour, 1 cup of granulated sugar, two teaspoons of baking powder, and 1/4 teaspoon of baking soda. Once mixed, the mixture can be stored in an airtight container. Three ounces of this mix or about six tablespoons can be added to a cake mix to achieve 18.25 ounces of dry ingredients. To make a chocolate cake, reduce the all-purpose flour to 1 cup plus three tablespoons, and add five tablespoons of unsweetened cocoa powder to the mix. This addition to a cake mix will result in a successful cake when baking a vintage recipe.

Several words used in the recipes required research to determine their meaning, some requiring a leap of faith. For example, finding cutter milk in a vintage recipe caused a lot of confusion. Since cutter wasn't mentioned anywhere, an educated guess determined that cutter was likely a typo. Not surprisingly, baking the cake with buttermilk yielded an excellent finished product.

The most curious discovery while studying the recipes was that *recipes* were once called *receipts*! The word *receipts* is derived from the old French word *recite*, which means a receipt, recipe, or prescription. Merriam-Webster notes that a *receipt*, documenting receiving goods or money, began in the 16th century. By the 17th century, both *receipt* and *recipe* referred to cooking instructions. Today, using the word *receipt* to refer to cooking instructions is archaic. Still, the use of both words lasted until the latter part of the 20th century in the United States, especially in the Southern states. Webster noted an amusing play on words--receiving a *receipt* or a *recipe* is exchanging something valuable from one person to another, for an excellent recipe is indeed a treasure!

Diffusion Throughout the Community:

Crockett has a long history of organizations publishing community cookbooks as fundraisers. Finding vintage community cookbooks at the All-Town Garage Sale held in May every year is considered a find. Over the years, many residents have collected or inherited several vintage volumes, and there is a collection at the Crockett Historical Museum. The community cookbooks date from about 1937 through 1993 and were compiled by organizations such as the Italian Catholic Federation, The St. Rose Women's Guild, the Chamber of Commerce, and the Friends of the Library, to name just a few organizations. C&H Sugar has also published several cookbooks. Thumbing through several community cookbooks' tattered, ingredient-stained pages yielded the same recipes in Louise Magnaghi's cake recipe collection.

This discovery led to how the cake recipes might have been diffused and shared throughout the community. Did the recipes in the community cookbooks come from the working women in the refinery, or did they originate from other sources within the community? These questions led to exploring the genesis of community cookbooks published nationwide.

Most community cookbooks in the United States began as a way for women to raise funds to achieve a common goal. Because opportunities to generate income were limited for women, they were resourceful. Women used what they knew, cooking and baking, and what they had access to, the kitchen, to further their causes. The first community cookbook published in the United States is attributed to Maria J. Moss in 1864. Ms. Moss led the effort to compile and sell a cookbook to subsidize the medical costs of Union soldiers injured in the Civil War and support their families. Protestant churchwomen completed the book. The first known community cookbook on the West Coast was published in San Francisco in 1872. As noted in the cookbook, it was compiled by and dedicated to "the ladies of the First Congregational Church."

Besides being a fundraising tool documenting individual members' cuisine, community cookbooks were also political pamphlets that reflected an area's historical accounts and political views. One such example is the *Woman Suffrage Cookbook*, published between 1886 and 1920 when the 19th Amendment was ratified to the U.S. Constitution, granting white women the right to vote. The *Woman Suffrage Cookbook* is still available today. It includes recipes from notable women, including Louisa May Alcott and other women breaking gender barriers in their professions. Its pages are peppered, pun intended, with pro-suffrage quotes and philosophy. Although black women worked in the Women's Suffrage movement, they weren't given the right to vote until the Civil Rights Legislation advocated by President Lyndon B. Johnson was passed by Congress in 1964. The Voting Rights Act followed in 1965.

Today, community cookbooks are an essential research

tool for culinary historians and historians in general. The United States Library of Congress provides an online catalog of digitized community cookbooks across the United States. The cookbooks reflect the communities that produced them and document the social structure of an area by including certain people and traditions while excluding others. They are extraordinary documents that provide records of regional culinary cultures and historical, philosophical, and religious backgrounds.

The similarities between the community cookbooks and Louise Magnaghi's recipe collection can't be ignored from a women's studies perspective. Like the community cookbooks, the cake recipes exchanged and shared by the women in the refinery represent the cuisine of this specific group of women who lived and worked together in their unique town, Crockett. The recipes reflect their shared values and traditions and provide insight into their food preferences. For those recipe writers who were immigrants and first-generation immigrant daughters, these recipes offer an insight into their degree of assimilation to American culture; that is, baking American cakes popular for their time was a priority. It was surprising to find only one Italian cake recipe in the entire collection, a German cake recipe shared by a Portuguese woman and a generic American cake shared by a woman of Mexican descent. Were traditional ethnic recipes specific to particular cultural groups only baked and eaten at home with the family? Was this a result of societal pressures to assimilate, fit in, and become a part of the great United States melting pot? Or was it because these ethnic recipes weren't written down? These old-world cultural recipes were likely made at home repeatedly from memory, perhaps under the watchful eyes of a *nonna,* 'grandmother.'

As it became apparent that the cake recipes and community cookbooks were a form of self-expression, pride, and identity for the women, the significance of the recipes individually and as a group came into sharper focus. Women in the refinery expressed themselves through their doing, using their hands, cooking, baking, and working. With this keener understanding, it is easy to surmise why the women in the refinery supported and pushed the young college-bound women to attend college. Simply put, they wanted the young women summer hires to do the things they couldn't. This encouragement was a powerful example of the female generational support common among Crockett immigrant mothers, aunts, friends, neighbors, and grandparents.

After gaining these insights and examining the Crockett Community Cookbooks, it was found that many recipes in the collection were listed multiple times throughout the cookbooks. Some recipes were attributed to the same women noted in Louise Magnaghi's recipe collection; however, several recipe writers claimed the recipe as their own, making it impossible to know who the original author was. The vintage from-scratch recipes in the community cookbooks can be baked today; however, those that use cake mixes require adjustments and correction, such as using the cake mix additives included herein for a successful bake. Some bakers modernized vintage recipes, such as the Booze Cake recipe, using cake mixes instead of baking from scratch—perhaps their meaning of homemade shifted from baking a scratch cake to just baking at home.

After the conclusion of the recipe investigation, some, but not all, of the three questions can be answered. First, a chronological recipe timeline was developed using documentation methods, ingredients, and various techniques. Secondly, after testing the recipes in a home kitchen, one can conclude that some but not all of their ingredients and techniques were unique to the age at which the recipe was written. A clear progression of cake baking techniques and how food technology affected baking methods and ingredients over time became evident; modifications and adjustments were made to ingredients and techniques for today's bakers. The final question of how the recipes were shared throughout the community couldn't be answered definitively. It couldn't be determined where the recipes originated or what came first –- the sharing in the Locker Room or the recipes published in the Crockett Community Cookbooks. However, this collection of cake recipes was undeniably important to the women in the Locker Room.

While writing this book, the importance of these recipes became even more evident through the many discussions among Crockett residents. On one such occasion, a Crockett resident mentioned that the Coffee Cake Manele originated with her aunt, who baked it often. Yet, the collection attributes this special local cake to the mother of Mary, one of the women working at the refinery. Mary had shared the recipe at the refinery with her mother's name and a date, 1957, written on the recipe. On another occasion, while testing and researching a recipe, one of the daughters of a woman who had shared the recipe at the refinery could no longer find her copy. Happily, this treasured family recipe was returned to her.

~

I hope that you will enjoy baking and serving these cakes. Wouldn't it be wonderful if the cakes help you recall a happy day, a past celebration, an event in your life, or perhaps just a happy memory of having shared it with someone you love?

Enjoy!

Ciambella

Makes one large round pound cake

Ciambella, 'ring' in Italian, refers to various ring-shaped baked goods in multiple sizes, from donuts to full-sized cakes. An old Italian proverb states: *non tutte le ciambelle riescono col buco*, 'things can't be expected to turn out right every time.' This was never truer than when testing this cake. It took multiple bakes and research to determine that a critical ingredient, milk, had been omitted from the recipe.

In Italy, the *ciambella* is enjoyed at breakfast with a *cappuccino* or as a snack cake throughout the day. This recipe isn't found in any of the Crockett community cookbooks. It is likely a family cake baked repeatedly in a Valona immigrant kitchen.

For the cake:
One cube of unsalted butter melted
2-1/2 cups all-purpose flour
2-1/2 teaspoons of baking powder
1/2 teaspoon salt
Glazed fruit or raisins (optional)
Four large eggs

217

1-3/4 cups granulated sugar
1/4 cup vegetable oil
2-1/2 teaspoons vanilla
1/2 cup milk

Make the cake:
Grease and flour a two-quart round tube pan, such as an angel food or Bundt pan. Preheat the oven to 350 degrees F. Melt the butter and set it aside to cool. In a separate bowl, combine the flour, baking powder, and salt with a fork and set this mixture aside. If adding glazed fruit or raisins, mix them with one tablespoon of the flour mixture and set them aside.

Whisk together the eggs and sugar, and then add the vegetable oil, vanilla, and melted butter until the mixture becomes light and frothy. Alternately, add the dry ingredients and milk to the egg mixture. Add the raisins and glazed fruits if using them. Pour the batter into the prepared pan and bake for forty-five minutes.

Check if the cake is made by inserting a toothpick in the center until it comes out clean. Leave the cake in the pan to cool for fifteen minutes, then turn it onto a cooking rack and let it cool completely.

Notes:
Serve the Ciambella simply as a snack cake. As a dessert cake, dust it with powdered sugar and serve it with berries, gelato, sorbet, ice cream, or whipped cream sweetened with powdered sugar flavored with vanilla extract.

Cinnamon Supper Cake

Makes one 8" round or square cake

A small effort is required to bake this vintage cake, which yields an astonishingly tasty result. It is likely called a supper cake because it is the perfect snack in the evening after a big meal. It is best right out of the oven. Served with coffee or tea, it is perfection!

While the history of this vintage cinnamon supper cake remains a mystery, its unique charm is undeniable. It's a cake that was perhaps born out of necessity, using simple pantry staples. Despite not being featured in Crockett community cookbooks, its simplicity and flavor make it a must-try for any baker.

For the cake:
1 cup sifted all-purpose flour
1-1/2 teaspoons of baking powder
1/4 teaspoon salt
1/4 cup unsalted butter
3/4 cup granulated sugar
One egg

One teaspoon of vanilla extract
1/2 cup milk

For the topping:
Three tablespoons of powdered sugar
One teaspoon of ground cinnamon
One tablespoon of soft, unsalted butter

Make the cake:
Preheat the oven to 375 degrees F. Grease and flour the cake pan and set it aside. Mix and sift the flour, baking powder, and salt and set aside. Cream the butter and sugar until light and fluffy, about four minutes. Add the egg, vanilla extract, and milk and beat until smooth. Add the dry ingredients to the butter mixture and beat until smooth.

Pour the batter into the pan and bake it for 20-25 minutes. While the cake is in the oven, prepare the topping by sifting the powdered sugar and cinnamon. Once the cake is done, check with a toothpick. It should come out clean. Take it out of the oven, spread it with soft butter, and sprinkle the cinnamon-sugar topping. Serve the cake warm or at room temperature for a delightful treat.

Dark Fruit Cake

Makes two loaf-pan fruit cakes

This recipe, popular in Crockett in the late 1920s and early 1930s, is well over one hundred years old. It was made in the Carquinez Grammar School home economics student kitchens on the third floor, where girls were taught to be homemakers. While the Crockett community cookbooks contain several fruit cake recipes, this particular recipe was not found.

For the cake:
1 pound citron, chopped
1 pound raisins
1 pound currants
1/2 pound walnuts or blanched almonds, chopped
1 cup butter
2 cups brown sugar
Six eggs
1/4 cup fruit juice or whiskey
2 cups all-purpose flour
One teaspoon of baking powder

One teaspoon salt
One teaspoon mace
1/2 teaspoon cloves
1/2 teaspoon nutmeg
1/2 teaspoon allspice
One teaspoon cinnamon

Make the cake:

Start by preparing the pans. Line two 7-1/2" x 3-1/2" loaf pans with baking parchment and grease them well. Preheat the oven to 250 degrees F. Soften the citron by heating it in a double boiler or oven, then chop it. If you prefer smaller fruit pieces, chop the raisins and currants and mix them with the citron. Finally, chop the nuts and add them to the dried fruit mixture.

Sift the flour once before measuring. Once measured, use a tablespoon of flour to dredge the dried fruit and nuts. Mix well. Add the baking powder, salt, and spices to the remaining flour and set the mixture aside.

Cream the butter and the sugar until light and creamy. Beat the eggs with a fork and add the well-beaten eggs, flour mixture, fruit juice, or whiskey alternately to the creamed shortening and sugar. Add the dried fruit/nuts mixture to the batter, ensuring the fruit and nuts are distributed evenly throughout.

Spread the mixture evenly in the pans and place them in a slow oven. This slow baking process, lasting about two hours, is crucial for the cake's rich flavor and moist texture. At the one-and-one-half-hour mark, check if the cake is made by inserting a toothpick in the center. If it comes out clean, the cake is ready. Remove the cakes from the oven and let them rest in the pan for fifteen minutes before transferring them to a rack to cool completely. Cool the cakes completely before slicing.

Eggless Spice Cake

Makes a 9″ round cake or a 13″ x 15″ rectangular cake

This simple vintage one-bowl snack cake can be easily made if short on eggs. Moist and spicey on its own, the nuts and raisins can be omitted to create an even simpler cake. The streusel-type topping finishes the cake off nicely.

The Eggless Spice Cake wasn't found in any Crockett community cookbooks. It falls into the make-do category popular during the World Wars and the Depression, when ingredients such as eggs, butter, and milk were expensive, rationed, or challenging to find.

For the cake:
3 cups all-purpose flour
1-1/2 cups granulated sugar
Two cubes of unsalted butter
One teaspoon of ground cloves
One teaspoon of ground cinnamon
One teaspoon of ground nutmeg
One teaspoon salt
1 cup nuts, chopped or ground (optional)

1 cup raisins (optional)
1-1/2 cups buttermilk
1-1/2 teaspoons baking soda

Make the cake:

Grease and flour a 9" springform or rectangular cake pan and set it aside. Preheat the oven to 350 degrees F. Process the flour, sugar, and unsalted butter in a food processor as if making a pie crust. Set aside 1/2 cup of this mixture to sprinkle on the cake before baking.

To the flour/sugar/butter mixture, add the cloves, cinnamon, nutmeg, and salt and mix well. If using, add the nuts and raisins. Combine the buttermilk and the baking soda. Stir the buttermilk mixture into the dry mixture and mix well. Transfer the mixture to the cake pan and sprinkle the top with the streusel topping.

Bake for 45 minutes, checking for doneness every five minutes, until fully baked. Cool the cake in the pan for 15 minutes, then remove it and cool it on a wire rack.

Notes:

Grind the nuts to create an even texture. Bake the cake in a 9" springform pan so it can be easily removed without disturbing the streusel topping.

Filled Coffee Cake Manele

Makes a two-layer 8″ or 9″ cake

The Filled Coffee Cake Manele has likely been the most popular cake in Crockett over the years. Its popularity is evidenced by its recipe being included in several Crockett community cookbooks submitted by different women.

For the topping:
1/2 cup brown sugar
One tablespoon of sifted all-purpose flour
One teaspoon of ground cinnamon
1/2 cup chopped nuts

For the filling:
1 cup milk
1/3 cup sifted all-purpose flour
1 cup granulated sugar
One large egg, beaten
One teaspoon vanilla
1/2-pint heavy whipping cream, whipped

For the Cake:
1/2 cup unsalted butter
1 cup granulated sugar
Two large eggs
Two teaspoons of vanilla extract
2 cups sifted all-purpose flour
1/2 teaspoon salt
Four teaspoons of baking powder
3/4 cup whole milk

Make the filling:
Sift the flour and sugar together. Scald the milk in a double boiler and slowly add the sifted flour and sugar. Cook the mixture until thick, stirring constantly. Add one beaten egg and cook until the custard is set. Add the vanilla and place the cooked custard in a bowl, covering it with plastic wrap to prevent skin from forming on the top. Refrigerate until cool. Before assembling the cake, whip the cream and fold it into the cold custard.

Make the cake:
Coat two cake pans with shortening. Cut a round of parchment paper for the bottom of the cake pans and place it in the pans. Grease and flour the pans and parchment paper. Preheat the oven to 350 degrees F.

Mix the topping and set it aside. Sift the flour, salt, and baking powder together.

Cream the butter and granulated sugar until light and fluffy, about four minutes. Separate the eggs and place the egg whites aside. Slightly beat the egg yolks and add them to the creamed butter mixture. Beat slightly. Add the flour and baking powder mixture alternately with the milk. Add the vanilla extract.

In the clean bowl of an electric mixer, beat the egg whites and fold these into the batter.

Spread the batter evenly into the two prepared cake pans and sprinkle each with the topping mixture. Bake the cake in a moderate oven for 20 to 25 minutes. Check for doneness by inserting a toothpick in the center of the cake until the toothpick comes out clean. Let the layers rest in the pans for 15 minutes before removing them. Cool the layers on racks.

When the cake is cold, slice each layer horizontally and fill the layers with the custard filling. Refrigerate the cake, but bring it to room temperature before serving.

Notes:

This cake can be baked in 8" or 9" pans. Always use a double boiler to achieve the proper custard texture. Pass the custard through a sieve to ensure there are no lumps. Cool the cake thoroughly before slicing and filling the layers.

French Cream Cake

Makes a two-layer, 8" cake

A rich, creamy, butter, vanilla-flavored custard sand-wiched between four soft, moist sponge layers elevate this cake into a memorable celebration cake. Sprinkled with powdered sugar, the cake is delicious, simple, understated, and elegant. The recipe wasn't found in any Crockett community cookbooks.

For the custard:
Two large eggs
3/4 cup granulated sugar
Two tablespoons cornstarch
2 cups of milk
One tablespoon grated lemon or orange rind
1/2 teaspoon vanilla
1/2 cup of unsalted butter (one cube)

For the cake
2-1/4 cups cake flour
1-1/2 teaspoons baking powder
One teaspoon salt

Three tablespoons water
Five large eggs
1-1/2 cups granulated sugar
One teaspoon of vanilla extract

Make the custard:

Make the custard first so it has plenty of time to cool. The recipe makes about three cups.

Beat the eggs slightly and add the sugar and cornstarch. Add the milk to the egg mixture and cook, stirring with a whisk, over boiling water until the mixture is thick and coats the back of a spoon. Add the grated lemon or orange rind and the vanilla. Add the butter, stirring until smooth. Remove the mixture from the heat. Place plastic wrap on the custard and cool it completely in the refrigerator.

Make the cake:

Make sure all ingredients are at room temperature. Coat the cake pans with shortening. Cut a round of parchment paper for the bottom of the cake pans and place it in the pans. Grease the cake pans and the parchment paper and set them aside. Preheat the oven to 350 degrees F.

Sift the cake flour, measure it, and then sift it again with the baking powder and salt. Add the water to the eggs in the bowl of a stand mixer and beat them for about 5 minutes until they are very light. Gradually add the sugar and continue beating for an additional 5 minutes. Fold the flour mixture into the egg mixture carefully to not deflate the batter.

Pour the batter evenly into the prepared pans and bake for 20 to 25 minutes. Start checking the cake at 20 minutes, and do not overbake. Check for doneness by inserting a toothpick in the center of the cake until the toothpick comes out clean.

Let the cake cool in the pans for 15 minutes, then remove it. Remove the parchment paper and let it cool on a cake rack. After the cake is cool, split each layer in half and remove the top or crown of one of the layers, ensuring the layers are flat and of the same height. To assemble the cake, spread one cup of custard on top of each layer and secure the cake with two skewers. Quickly put the cake into the refrigerator, allowing the layers to absorb the custard and set. Once the cake is set, remove the skewers and sprinkle the top with powdered sugar.

Notes:

It's best to start by making the custard ahead of time and letting it cool. Adding blueberries or thinly sliced strawberries would make a delicious summer cake!

Gugelhupf

Makes one Bundt cake

The Gugelhopf is an impressive buttery sponge cake, a delicious celebration cake perfect for any occasion. While the Gugelhopf, also known as a "Kugelhopf," is typically a yeast-based brioche-type cake, this recipe uses baking powder for leavening.

This recipe isn't found in any Crockett community cookbooks. Still, several conversations with Crockett residents revealed that it was a memorable cake, enjoyed mainly on the east side of town. I finished the cake with a dusting of powdered sugar.

For the cake:
1-1/2 cups sifted all-purpose flour
1/2 teaspoon salt
Two teaspoons of baking powder
1 cup unsalted butter at room temperature
2 cups granulated sugar
Six eggs at room temperature, separated
Six tablespoons whole milk

233

Choice of flavoring:
One teaspoon vanilla, 1/2 teaspoon almond extract, or two teaspoons grated lemon

Make the cake:
Make sure all ingredients are at room temperature. Grease and flour a 12-cup Gugelhupf pan (also called a Turk's head mold). Preheat the oven to 350 degrees F.

Combine the flour, salt, and baking powder. Mix it thoroughly with a fork and set it aside.

Combine the milk and the flavoring and set the mixture aside. Cream the butter to the consistency of mayonnaise. Add the sugar slowly while continuing to cream the butter. Beat until light and fluffy, about four minutes. Beat in the egg yolks one at a time.

Add the flour and milk to the butter mixture, alternating each and stirring gently but thoroughly. Add the egg whites to a clean electric mixer bowl and beat until stiff but not dry. Fold the egg whites thoroughly into the batter. Pour the batter into the well-greased Gugelhupf pan.

Bake the cake for 45-55 minutes until it tests done. Check for doneness by inserting a toothpick in the center. When the toothpick comes out clean, the cake is done. Cool the cake in the pan for 10 minutes.

Loosen the cake gently around the rim and tube and invert it on a cake rack, allowing it to cool completely. Dust the cake with powdered sugar and garnish with whole maraschino cherries if desired.

Margaret's Rich Chocolate Cake

Makes a two-layer 8" or 9" cake; or a 13" x 9" sheet cake

This cake is an intensely flavored, moist, dense, rich chocolate cake with an equally flavored creamy filling. Dust the top with powdered sugar and serve it with a generous spoonful of vanilla ice cream, a dollop of heavy cream, or crème Fraiche. This recipe wasn't found in any of the Crockett community cookbooks.

For the cake:
1 cup natural cocoa powder, sifted
2/3 cup granulated sugar
1/2 cup room-temperature water
One teaspoon of baking soda
1 cup granulated sugar
1/2 cup unsalted butter
1/2 teaspoon salt
Three large eggs separated
2 cups all-purpose flour
One teaspoon of baking powder
2/3 cup water

For the frosting:
1 cup natural cocoa powder, sifted
1 cup granulated sugar
Three tablespoons corn starch
2 cups of water
One tablespoon butter
One teaspoon of vanilla extract

Make the cake:
Make sure all ingredients are at room temperature. Pre-heat the oven to 350 degrees F. Coat the cake pans with shortening. Cut a round piece of parchment paper for the bottom of the cake pans and place these in the pans. Grease and coat the cake pans and the parchment paper with cocoa powder and set them aside.

Place 1/2 cup water and 2/3 cup granulated sugar in a small saucepan and bring it to a boil. Remove the pan from the heat and add the cocoa powder, whisking the mixture until the cocoa powder has melted. Cover with plastic wrap and cool to room temperature. Add one teaspoon of baking soda to the mixture.

Separate the eggs. Cream 1 cup granulated sugar and 1/2 cup butter for four minutes. Add the egg yolks, one at a time, and mix between each addition.

Sift the flour and baking powder together, and add this mixture to the creamed butter, mixing alternately with 2/3 cup water. Add the chocolate mixture.

Add the egg whites to a clean electric mixer bowl, beat until stiff, and fold them into the batter. Pour the batter evenly into the prepared cake pans. Bake for 25 to 30 minutes. Check for doneness by inserting a toothpick in the center of the cake until the toothpick comes out clean. The cake should be cooled in the pans for 10 minutes, removed from the pans and parchment paper, and completely cooled on cooling racks.

Make the frosting:
Sift the cocoa powder and cornstarch. Mix the cocoa powder, sugar, cornstarch, and water and cook on top of a double boiler until it is thick, about 20-25 minutes, stirring occasionally. Remove the mixture from the heat and add one tablespoon of butter and one teaspoon of vanilla. Cover the mixture with plastic wrap and cool completely before using.

To assemble the cake, slice the layers in two, making a four-layer cake. Fill the cake and dust the top with powdered sugar.

Notes:
Make this cake using good-quality cocoa powder, as the quality of the cocoa powder will affect the cake's flavor.

Mayonnaise Cake

Makes a two-layer 8" or 9" cake

The Mayonnaise Cake is a Depression-era cake thought to have been invented by Best Foods/Hellmann's as an economical way to substitute mayonnaise for butter, milk, or thickened dairy products such as sour cream or buttermilk. The earliest printed recipe for this cake was found in the *Oakland Tribune*, dated March 7, 1927.

The Mayonnaise Cake was popular in Crockett as its recipe was included in three Crockett community cookbooks as early as 1976 and 1997.

For the cake:
1 cup pitted prunes, chopped
1 cup nuts, chopped or ground
One teaspoon of baking soda
1 cup boiling water
2 cups all-purpose flour
Three tablespoons unsweetened cocoa powder
1/2 teaspoon ground cinnamon
1/2 teaspoon salt

1 cup granulated sugar
1 cup mayonnaise
One teaspoon of vanilla extract

Make the cake:
Preheat the oven to 350 degrees F. Coat the cake pans with shortening. Cut a piece of parchment paper for the bottom of the cake pans and place these in the pans. Grease and coat the cake pans and the parchment paper with cocoa powder and set them aside.

Chop or grind the nuts and prunes together, then add the baking soda. Pour the boiling water over the mixture and set it aside to cool. Mix and sift the flour, cocoa powder, cinnamon, and salt into a small bowl. Mix the sugar and mayonnaise. Add the nut/prune mixture and the flour mixture, and add the vanilla extract. Stir well.

Pour the batter into the pans and bake for 20-25 minutes. Check for doneness by inserting a toothpick in the center of the cake until the toothpick comes out clean. Cool the cake in the pans for 10 minutes, then remove the cakes from the pans and the parchment paper. Cool the cake on cooling racks.

Notes:
For a fun variation, frost the cake with vanilla buttercream and sprinkle with mini chocolate chips. Grind the nuts and dates together to achieve an even texture without a crunch.

Orange Slice Cake

Makes a large, moist, flavorful pound cake

This vintage recipe yields a dense, moist pound cake with a light, refreshing orange glaze. Full of moisture and flavor, it is lighter than a fruit cake. The cake is best baked a day or two before serving to allow the deep orange flavor to develop.

This versatile cake can be served as a celebration cake during the fall or the holidays or as a hearty snack. Serve it as a snack or after dinner with creamy cheese such as Brie or a mild cream, farmer's, or mascarpone cheese—dust with confectioners' sugar.

This recipe wasn't in any Crockett community cookbooks. It was baked frequently for visiting C&H Sugar executives and served at the Guest Cottage.

For the cake:
3-1/2 cups sifted all-purpose flour
1/2 teaspoon salt
1-pound candied orange slices or candied orange peel, diced
8 ounces pitted dates, chopped or ground

2 cups chopped walnuts or pecans, chopped or ground
1 cup unsalted butter (2 cubes)
2 cups granulated sugar
Four large eggs, well-beaten
One teaspoon of baking soda
1/2 cup buttermilk

For the glaze:
1/2 cup orange juice
cup powdered sugar

Make the cake:
Prepare a sizeable 12-cup tube pan, such as an angel food cake pan or Bundt pan, by buttering and flouring the bottom and sides. Preheat the oven to 300 degrees F.

Sift the all-purpose flour and the salt, reserving 1/2 cup, and set it aside. Combine the chopped candied orange slices (or peel), dates, and nuts, and sprinkle with 1/2 cup of flour. Mix well.

Cream the butter and sugar until light and fluffy, about four minutes. Add the well-beaten eggs and mix well. Combine the baking soda and the buttermilk and gradually combine the butter, flour, and buttermilk, alternating each ingredient to achieve a creamy cake batter. Mix well and add the nut mixture.

Pour the batter into a large tube pan and bake for approximately 1 hour and 30 minutes. Check for doneness by inserting a toothpick in the center of the cake until it comes out clean.

Remove the cake from the oven and make the glaze by combining the orange juice and powdered sugar. Prick the cake with a toothpick to make holes for the glaze to penetrate. Pour the glaze over the hot cake and allow it to cool for about 15 minutes. Remove the cake from the pan and continue to cool it on a rack. Serve the cake when it is completely cool.

Potato Cake

Makes an 8" two-layer cake

This vintage cake is gluten-free because it's made with potato starch flour. Potato starch is a fine-grind flour made from dehydrated potatoes. It is often mixed with other flours to provide a more neutral flavor. The potato flour in this recipe imparts a soft texture, sweet and earthy flavor, and a crisp crust. Bake the cake a day before serving to allow all the flavors to develop fully.

The Potato Cake was once popular in Crockett and Valona and was included in three Crockett community cookbooks.

For the cake:
Six large eggs separated
1 cup granulated sugar
3/4 cup potato flour
One teaspoon of baking powder
Pinch of salt
Two teaspoons of vanilla or lemon extract

For the filling and frosting:
1-pint heavy whipping cream
One tablespoon of powdered sugar
One teaspoon of vanilla or lemon extract
Fresh fruit (berries, bananas, or pineapple) or strawberry jam

Make the cake:
Coat the cake pans with shortening. Cut a round piece of parchment paper for the bottom of the cake pans and place these in the pans. Grease and coat the cake pans and the parchment paper with flour and set them aside. Preheat the oven to 350 degrees F.

Mix the potato flour, baking powder, and salt and set this mixture aside. In a clean bowl of an electric mixer, beat the egg whites until stiff, gradually adding 1/2 cup of granulated sugar. Set the egg whites aside.

Using the same beater, beat the yolks for ten minutes until creamy. The cake will be fluffier the more the egg yolks are beaten. Gradually add 1/2 cup of granulated sugar and beat until smooth. Add two teaspoons of vanilla or lemon extract. Gradually hand fold the beaten egg whites into the egg yolks alternately with the dry mixture. Mix well.

Pour the batter into two 8" cake pans and bake for 20-25 minutes. Check for doneness by inserting a toothpick in the center of the cake until done. Let the cake cool in the pan for 15 minutes, then turn the cakes onto a baking rack and cool completely.

Make the filling and frosting:
Beat the cream with the powdered sugar and vanilla or lemon extract. To assemble the cake, spread the layers with whipped cream. Dust the top with confectioner sugar and serve.

Notes:

An alternate way to finish this cake is to spread a layer of your favorite jam on the bottom layer and then a layer of vanilla buttercream. Pipe the layer's edge with buttercream, then place a layer on top. Finish the edge of the top layer with buttercream stars. Vanilla-flavored buttercream and apricot jam would be a fabulous combination.

Prune Cake

Makes a 13" x 15" cake

This vintage recipe combines cocoa powder and stewed prunes to yield a moist, fragrant cake with a complex flavor. A versatile snack or informal cake, the prune cake can be elevated to a party cake when served with ice cream, gelato, or flavored whipped cream. It was found in two Crockett community cookbooks and *Crockett Cookery*, published by the Carquinez Women's Club in 1937.

For the cake:
3 cups all-purpose flour
One teaspoon of ground nutmeg
1-1/2 teaspoons ground cinnamon
Three tablespoons cocoa powder
One teaspoon of baking powder
Two teaspoons of baking soda
Pinch of salt
2 cups brown sugar
1/2 cup unsalted butter (one stick)
Three large eggs, well-beaten
One teaspoon of vanilla extract

cup stewed prunes, pitted and roughly chopped
1 cup prune syrup

Make the cake:
Preheat the oven to 350 degrees F. Coat the cake pan with shortening. Cut a piece of parchment paper for the bottom of the cake pans. Grease and coat the cake pan and the parchment paper with flour and set it aside.

Place the prunes in a saucepan with 1-1/2 cups of water. Bring to a boil, reduce the heat, cover, and cook the prunes for ten minutes. Remove the pan from the heat and let cool. Drain the prunes, reserving the remaining liquid (syrup). Pit the prunes, chop them roughly, and set them aside. Measure the syrup and add water to make one cup of liquid.

Combine the flour, nutmeg, cinnamon, cocoa powder, baking powder, baking soda, and salt, and set the mixture aside. Cream the butter and brown sugar until fluffy, about four minutes. Then, add the beaten eggs and the vanilla extract. Mix well. Alternately, add the flour mixture with the prune syrup and beat well. Mix in the chopped prunes by hand.

Spread the cake batter into the prepared pan and smooth the top with an offset spatula.

Bake for 35 to 40 minutes. Check for doneness by inserting a toothpick in the center of the cake until the toothpick comes out clean. Cool the cake in the pan for fifteen minutes, then turn it onto a cooling rack to cool completely.

Dust the cake with powdered sugar and serve with vanilla ice cream or sweetened whipped cream.

Notes:
Add one cup of chocolate chips to the batter before baking to make a festive variation.

Raw Apple Cake

Makes a 7" x 12" rectangular cake or a 4-1/2" x 11-1/2" loaf

This versatile vintage cake is moist, sweet, and tasty. It can be served as a snack or breakfast cake. It is also delicious, served with vanilla ice cream, heavy whipping cream flavored with powdered sugar and vanilla, or just dusted with powdered sugar. The apples enhance the cake's texture by adding moisture and sweetness.

Three Crockett Community Cookbooks included the Raw Apple Cake, making it a popular cake in Crockett and Valona.

For the cake:
4 cups raw apples, chopped (about four large apples, any variety)
2 cups all-purpose flour
Two teaspoons of ground cinnamon
1/2 teaspoon salt
Two teaspoons of baking soda
2 cups granulated sugar
1/2 cup vegetable oil

Two large eggs
Two teaspoons vanilla
2 cups chopped or ground walnuts (optional)

Make the cake:

Preheat the oven to 350 degrees F. Coat the cake pan with shortening. Cut a piece of parchment paper for the bottom of the cake pan and place it in the pan. Grease and coat the cake pan and the parchment paper with flour and set it aside.

Peel, slice, and chop the apples and set them aside. Sift the flour, cinnamon, salt, and baking soda. If using walnuts, flour them with one tablespoon of the measured flour and set them aside. Beat the eggs, sugar, oil, and vanilla with a fork and add this mixture to the chopped apples.

Add the dry ingredients to the wet mixture and blend well. The batter will appear dry, but don't add any liquid. Pour the batter into the cake pan and bake for 60-70 minutes. Check for doneness by inserting a toothpick in the center of the cake until the toothpick comes out clean.

Cool the cake in the pan for 15 minutes, then remove it to a rack to cool completely before slicing.

Notes:

This cake bakes beautifully in a standard 7″ x 12″ two-quart rectangular pan. It can also be baked in a long loaf pan, 12 cm. x. 30cm., approximately 4-1/2″ x 11-1/2″. This pan size and shape enabled the cake to be baked evenly, resulting in smaller slices.

Squash Cake

Makes one loaf

This vintage snack cake combines the flavor of zucchini bread with that of a spice cake. The Squash Cake can also be called a quick bread as it can be made quickly by hand using only two bowls. Except for adding ground nutmeg, this cake resembles the Raw Apple Cake.

The Squash Cake was not included in any Crockett Community Cookbooks, perhaps because it was not meant to impress. It is simple and tasty, a staple cake meant to be enjoyed at home.

For the cake:
2 cups all-purpose flour
One teaspoon salt
Two teaspoons of ground cinnamon
One teaspoon nutmeg
Two teaspoons of baking soda
2 cups granulated sugar
Two large eggs
3/4 cup vegetable oil
4 cups chopped or shredded squash (such as zucchini or

yellow squash)

1 cup chopped or ground nuts (optional)

Make the cake:

Preheat the oven to 350 degrees F. Coat the cake pan with shortening. Cut a piece of parchment paper for the bottom of the cake pan. Grease and coat the cake pan and the parchment paper with flour and set it aside.

Shred the squash by hand to prevent the squash from making too much liquid. Set it aside. If using a food processor, drain the squash before using it. Combine and sift the flour, salt, cinnamon, nutmeg, and baking soda. Mix thoroughly and set the mixture aside. Beat the eggs lightly. Add the vegetable oil and the shredded squash and mix until blended.

Place the batter in the pan and bake it for one hour or until done. Check for doneness by inserting a toothpick in the center of the cake until it comes out clean. When fully baked, remove the pan from the oven and allow the cake to rest on a rack for 15 minutes. Remove the cake from the pan and cool it completely before slicing.

Notes:

The squash's high water content will affect the baking time. The sugar can be reduced to 1-1/2 cups without compromising the flavor or texture. Dust the top of the cake with powdered sugar before serving, or serve it with a dollop of flavored heavy whipped cream, ice cream, or gelato.

Wine Cake

Makes a 5" x 8" loaf

This vintage Wine Cake could be renamed Old Fashioned Spiced Apple Raisin Wine Cake. For the best flavor, bake this cake a day before serving so its deep spice flavor has time to develop. Serve it with white or dessert wine and dusted with powdered sugar. This recipe wasn't found in any Crockett community cookbooks.

For the cake:
1 cup water
1 cup raisins
Two tablespoons unsalted butter
2 cups all-purpose flour
1 cup granulated sugar
One teaspoon salt
One tablespoon of baking soda
One tablespoon of ground cinnamon
One tablespoon nutmeg
1/2 cup white wine
Two medium apples, sliced thin
1 cup nuts, chopped or ground

Make the cake:

Boil the water, raisins, and butter for five minutes, then cool the mixture. Preheat the oven to 350 degrees F. Coat the cake pan with shortening. Cut a piece of parchment paper for the bottom of the cake pan and place it in the pan. Grease and coat the cake pan and the parchment paper with flour and set it aside.

Mix and sift the flour, sugar, salt, baking soda, cinnamon, and nutmeg into a bowl. Add the cooled raisin mixture and the wine to the flour mixture. Blend well. If the batter seems dry, add white wine, up to 1/2 cup. Add the sliced apples and nuts and pour the batter into a prepared pan. Carefully press the mixture into the pan to remove any voids.

Bake for 1 hour or until done. Check for doneness by inserting a toothpick in the center of the cake until the toothpick comes out clean. Cool the cake on a rack for 15 minutes before removing the cake from the pan. Slice and serve when the cake is cool.

.

Anniversary Fiesta Cake

Makes an Angel Food Cake

The Anniversary Fiesta Cake is an impressive vintage celebration cake appropriate for any festive occasion. It is light and delicate, and the whipping cream carries the peanut brittle without being too sweet. This cake is a variation of the famous Blum's Coffee Crunch Cake, invented in San Francisco in the 1940s and became a Bay Area favorite. The only difference is that it uses peanut brittle rather than coffee-flavored crunch. The recipe for this cake wasn't found in any Crockett community cookbooks.

For the cake:
1-1/4 cups sifted cake flour
3/4 cup granulated sugar
1/2 cup egg yolks (about six large eggs)
1/4 cup cold water
One tablespoon of lemon juice
One teaspoon of vanilla extract
1 cup egg whites (about 7 or 8 large eggs)
One teaspoon of cream of tartar

One teaspoon salt
3/4 cups granulated sugar

For the frosting:
2 cups heavy whipping cream (one pint)
Two tablespoons granulated sugar
Two teaspoons of vanilla extract
Peanut brittle

Make the cake:
Preheat the oven to 350 degrees F. Line the bottom of a 10" diameter, 4" high tube (Angel Food) pan with parchment paper and set the pan aside.

Sift the cake flour, then measure and sift together the flour and 3/4 cup of granulated sugar. Add the flour/sugar mixture to an electric mixer bowl. Add the egg yolks, cold water, lemon juice, and vanilla extract to the center. Beat well until the mixture forms a smooth, moderately thick batter, about 4 minutes.

To make a meringue, add the egg whites, cream of tartar, and salt to a clean, large mixing bowl. Whip, using an electric mixer, until delicate foam forms throughout. Gradually add 3/4 cup of granulated sugar, two tablespoons at a time. Continue beating until the meringue is firm and forms straight peaks when the beater is gently lifted.

Pour the batter slowly over the meringue while gently folding it with a spatula. Fold the batter into the meringue until blended–do not stir. Gently pour the batter into an ungreased pan. Carefully cut through the batter, going around the tube 5 or 6 times with a knife to break large air bubbles. Make sure the batter is level in the pan.

Bake for 45-50 minutes or until the top springs back when lightly touched. Check for doneness by inserting a toothpick in the center until the toothpick comes out clean. Once the pan is out of the oven, immediately turn the pan over, placing the tube over the neck of a funnel or a bottle. Let the cake hang upside down until it has cooled.

Loosen the cake from the sides and the tube with a metal spatula or knife. Turn the pan over and hit the edge of the pan sharply to loosen. Place the cake on a cooling rack and remove the parchment paper when cooled.

Assemble the cake:

Cut the cake into four equal layers. Crush the peanut brittle using a plastic bag and a rolling pin and set it aside. Place the whipping cream, granulated sugar, and vanilla in a bowl and beat it until it holds its shape.

Spread about half the whipped cream between the layers and the remainder over the top and sides. Cover the cake gently, generously, and thoroughly with crushed peanut brittle. Refrigerate until a half-hour before serving.

Notes:

Add whipped cream and crushed peanut brittle between the layers to create a contemporary naked look. Frost the top only and leave the sides bare, ensuring the whipped cream between the layers comes right to the edge of the cake. Scrape the sides of the cake, removing any cream that remains. Before serving, add the crushed brittle to the top. The crunchy brittle on top adds a pleasant contrast to the brittle that has softened between the layers.

This would make a delicious summer cake by substituting blueberries or thinly sliced strawberries for peanut brittle.

Apple Dump Cake

Makes a 9" x 13" cake

This cake is perfect for a potluck or a big family gathering. It can be prepared from scratch using fresh apples or conveniently and quickly using canned apple pie filling. Either way, it is delicious and moist. This was a Crockett favorite as it was included in two community cookbooks.

The earliest reference to a Dump Cake is from a Duncan Hines publication from the 1980s. A traditional Dump Cake is prepared using a cake mix, dumping all the ingredients into a cake pan and baking it.

For the cake:
2 cups all-purpose flour
One teaspoon of baking soda
One teaspoon salt
Two teaspoons of ground cinnamon
2 cups granulated sugar
1 cup vegetable oil
Two eggs lightly beaten
One teaspoon of vanilla extract
21-ounce can of apple pie filling or the equivalent

amount of fresh sliced apples prepared as apple pie filling

Make the cake:

Preheat the oven to 375 degrees F. Make sure all ingredients are at room temperature. Coat the cake pan with shortening. Cut a piece of parchment paper for the bottom of the cake pan and place it in the pan. Grease and coat the cake pan and the parchment paper with flour and set it aside.

Combine and mix well the flour, soda, salt, and cinnamon. Set this mixture aside. Stir together the sugar, oil, eggs, and vanilla extract and mix well. Alternately, add the dry ingredients with 1/2 can of the apple pie filling to the wet ingredients. Add the nuts if using. Fold in the rest of the apple pie filling and mix lightly.

Spread the batter into the prepared pan and bake for 50-60 minutes. Check for doneness by inserting a toothpick in the center of the cake until it comes out clean.

Notes:

This cake can be finished with powdered sugar. It can also be served plain with sweetened heavy whipping cream, vanilla ice cream, or gelato.

Booze Cake

Makes one large Bundt Cake

This is a rich and moist vintage fall/winter holiday cake. It has a soft, sweet, and spicy texture and is best served the day after it is made. Prettily dusted with powdered sugar, it is best served with sweetened whipped cream, crème anglaise, or vanilla ice cream.

This cake was a favorite in Crockett and Valona, and it is included in Good Things to Eat, compiled by the Italian Catholic Federation Branch #14 in 1976. A slightly different version is included in *Crockett Cookery*, published by the Carquinez Women's Club in September 1939. Oddly, this cake is called a Booze Cake even though it has no liquor!

For the cake:
3 cups raisins
3 cups of water
Two teaspoons of baking soda
1 cup vegetable oil
Four large eggs
One teaspoon of vanilla extract
3 cups of all-purpose flour

1 cup brown sugar
1 cup granulated sugar
One teaspoon of ground cloves
One teaspoon salt
One teaspoon allspice
Two teaspoons of ground cinnamon
Three teaspoons of baking powder
1 cup chopped nuts

Make the cake:

Preheat the oven to 350 degrees F. Grease and flour a 9"
springform, two-quart Bundt pan, or Angel Food pan and
set it aside. Cut and grease a piece of parchment paper to fit
the bottom of the pan to ensure that the cake will release effortlessly.

Place the water and raisins in a saucepan and simmer for
ten minutes. Let the mixture cool, then add the baking soda
and the vegetable oil. Stir until combined.

Mix and sift all the dry ingredients and stir in the nuts.
Beat the eggs thoroughly and add to the raisin mixture. Add
the vanilla extract and mix well. Add the dry ingredients
and mix the batter well.

Pour the batter into the cake pan and bake for 60-70 minutes, checking for doneness at 60 minutes by inserting a
toothpick in the center of the cake. When the toothpick
comes out clean, the cake is done. When the cake is done,
remove it from the oven and rest in the pan for 15 minutes.
Turn the cake onto a cooling rack and cool it completely.

Notes:

Baking times will vary depending on humidity, ingredients, and the oven.

Chocolate Bavarian Torte

Makes a 9" layer cake

This impressive, delicious cake was served at the annual Bocce League Banquet at the Crockett Community Center in the fall. It isn't included in any Crockett Community Cookbooks.

For the cake:
One package of Devil's Food cake mix (without the pudding)

For the filling:
One 8-ounce package of cream cheese softened
2/3 cup packed light brown sugar
One teaspoon of vanilla extract
1/8 teaspoon salt
2 cups heavy whipping cream, whipped
Two tablespoons of grated chocolate

Make the cake:
Preheat the oven according to the package's instructions. Grease two 9" cake pans. Line the bottom of each pan with

parchment paper and grease the parchment paper so the cake won't stick to the pan.

Mix and bake the cake according to the package's instructions. Check for doneness by inserting a toothpick in the center of the cake until the toothpick comes out clean. Cool the cake in the pans on a rack for 15 minutes; remove it from the pans, remove the parchment paper, and cool it completely.

Beat the cream cheese in a mixing bowl, adding the sugar, vanilla, and salt until the mixture is light and fluffy. Beat the heavy cream until stiff peaks form, then fold the heavy cream into the cream cheese mixture. Split each layer and place the bottom layer on a serving dish. Spread the layer with 1/4 of the cream mixture, then sprinkle it with 1/4 of the grated chocolate. Repeat for the remaining layers.

Cover the cake and refrigerate it for at least 8 hours or overnight. Serve at room temperature.

Chocolate Cherry Bundt Cake

Makes one Bundt cake

This impressive contemporary, easy-to-make chocolaty cake is sweet and moist. The addition of cherry pie filling makes for a delicious, tart surprise.

For the cake:
18.25 ounces of chocolate cake mix, or 15.25 ounces of cake mix with an additional 3 ounces (or six tablespoons) of the blend noted in "Recipes."
One small 3.4-ounce instant chocolate pudding mix
Three large eggs at room temperature
1/2 cup vegetable oil
1 cup of water
21-ounce can of cherry pie filling

Make the cake:
Make sure all ingredients are at room temperature. Preheat the oven to 350 degrees F. Grease and coat the cake pan with flour and set it aside.

Combine the cake and pudding mixes, eggs, and vegetable oil in an electric mixer bowl. Slowly add the water

267

and beat for two minutes. Carefully fold in the cherry pie filling by hand, careful not to break up the cherries.

Pour the batter into a prepared Bundt pan and bake for 45 minutes to one hour or until done. Check for doneness by inserting a toothpick in the center of the cake until the toothpick comes out clean. Let the cake cool in the pan for 10 minutes, remove it, and place it on a cooling rack. When cool, dust it with powdered sugar and serve.

Notes:

Finish the cake with powdered sugar and serve it plain, with sweetened heavy whipped cream, vanilla ice cream, or gelato.

Chocolate Coconut Marshmallow Cake

Makes a two-layer, 8" cake

Marshmallows, chocolate, and sour cream make this a moist, rich, tasty cake. Coconut flakes toasted in butter add a nutty crunch, and cream cheese and powdered sugar make a frosting that transforms this cake into a decadent celebration cake.

For the cake:
16 marshmallows
3 ounces unsweetened chocolate
3/4 cup boiling water
2-1/4 cups all-purpose flour
1-1/2 teaspoons baking soda
1-1/2 teaspoons salt
Three large eggs
1-1/4 cups granulated sugar
One teaspoon of vanilla extract
1-1/2 cups sour cream

For the frosting:
Two tablespoons of unsalted butter

1 cup flaked coconut
1/3 cup unsalted butter, softened
6 ounces cream cheese, softened
1 pound powdered sugar
Two tablespoons milk
1/2 teaspoon vanilla extract

Make the cake:

Make sure all ingredients are at room temperature. Preheat the oven to 375 degrees F. Coat the cake pans with shortening. Cut a piece of parchment paper for the bottom of the cake pans and place them in the pan. Grease and coat the cake pan and the parchment paper with sifted cocoa powder and set them aside.

Melt the marshmallows and chocolate in a double boiler and add the boiling water. Beat until smooth, then let the mixture cool. Sift the flour, salt, and baking soda and set the mixture aside.

In a stand mixer bowl, beat the eggs until foamy, gradually adding the sugar until the mixture is thick. Add the vanilla extract and the chocolate mixture and mix thoroughly. Blend in the sour cream. Gradually add the dry ingredients and mix thoroughly.

Pour the batter into the cake pans and bake for 25-35 minutes. Check for doneness by inserting a toothpick in the center of the cake until the toothpick comes out clean. Cool the cake in the pans for 10 minutes, remove the layers, and cool thoroughly on racks.

Make the frosting:

Melt two tablespoons of butter in a saucepan. Add the flaked coconut and stir until golden brown. Remove the coconut from the heat and let it cool.

Cream 1/3 cup butter, add the cream cheese, and blend. Add a small amount of sugar and milk to the butter and cream cheese mixture, beating after each addition until all the sugar is incorporated. Add the vanilla extract and 3/4 cup of the toasted coconut.

Frost the cake, then sprinkle the remaining coconut on top.

Chocolate
Raisin
Applesauce
Cake

A two-layer 8" a 13"x 9" sheet cake; or a small bundt cake

Although eggless, this cake is moist and full of complex flavor. The added complexity of the ground nuts and raisins balances the combination of cocoa powder, cinnamon, nutmeg, and cloves. Grinding the nuts provides a depth of flavor without adding a crunchy texture to the cake, while melted butter and applesauce add moisture and richness. The chocolate cream cheese frosting, with its creamy texture and chocolate and vanilla flavors, can't be missed.

The applesauce cake originated in early colonial times in the New England Colonies of the United States. As it was diffused across the country, several variations in ingredients and shapes have emerged. Several recipes for applesauce cakes are included in Crockett community cookbooks, but they incorporate plain applesauce without adding cocoa powder.

For the cake:
1/2 cup (1 cube) unsalted butter, melted
2 cups all-purpose flour
1/2 teaspoon salt

273

1 cup granulated sugar
One tablespoon cornstarch
Three tablespoons unsweetened cocoa powder
One teaspoon of baking soda
One teaspoon of ground cinnamon
1/2 teaspoon ground nutmeg
1/2 teaspoon ground cloves
1 cup chopped or ground nuts
1 cup raisins
2 cups applesauce

For the frosting:
1-ounce unsweetened baker's chocolate melted
One 3-ounce package of cream cheese
2-1/2 cups sifted powdered sugar
One tablespoon milk

Make the cake:
Preheat the oven to 350 degrees F. Make sure all ingredients are at room temperature.

Coat the cake pan with shortening. Cut a piece of parchment paper for the bottom of the cake pan. Grease and coat the cake pan and the parchment paper with cocoa powder and set aside.

Melt the butter and let it cool. Mix and sift the flour, salt, sugar, cornstarch, cocoa powder, soda, cinnamon, nutmeg, and cloves into a bowl and set the mixture aside. Add the ground nuts, raisins, melted butter, and applesauce to the flour mixture. Mix well.

Pour the batter equally into the cake pans and bake. A small bundt cake should be baked in 45 minutes, an 8″ layer cake in about 25 minutes, and a 13″ x 9″ in about 35 minutes. Check for doneness by inserting a toothpick in the center until the toothpick comes out clean. Cool the cake in the pans for 15 minutes, then turn it onto a cooling rack and cool it completely.

Make the frosting, slice the layers in half, and frost the cake when sufficiently cooled.

Make the frosting:

Melt the unsweetened chocolate and let it cool completely. Sift the powdered sugar and cream it with the cream cheese. To the cream cheese mixture, add the cooled melted chocolate, the salt, the vanilla extract, and the milk. If the mixture is too stiff, add more milk. If the mixture is too runny, add more powdered sugar.

Notes:

Use good-quality cocoa powder to make this cake, as the cocoa powder's quality affects the cake's taste. Grind the nuts to add flavor complexity, not crunch, to the cake texture. A large grind is best. Pecans, almonds, or walnuts work best in this cake. For a contemporary look, make two 8" layers, splitting each layer and using the frosting to fill each. Leave the side bare, frost the top, and sprinkle it with chocolate shavings or mini chocolate chips.

Chocolate Sour Cream Kahlua Cake

Makes one Bundt cake

This cake is an easy-to-make, convenient "contemporary" cake made with a pre-packaged cake mix. Sour cream, Kahlua, and chocolate chips enhance the flavor of the cake mix, yielding a rich, moist cake full of flavor. This recipe wasn't found in any of the Crockett community cookbooks.

For the cake:
18.25-ounce devil's food cake mix or 15.25 ounces of cake mix with an additional 3 ounces (or six tablespoons) of the blend noted in "Recipes."
1 cup sour cream
1 cup Kahlua
3/4 cup vegetable or canola oil
Four large eggs

Make the cake:
Preheat the oven to 350 degrees F. Make sure all the ingredients are at room temperature. Butter a two-quart Bundt pan with melted butter and dust it with sifted cocoa powder. Set the pan aside.

Add all the ingredients to the bowl of an electric mixer and beat for 3-5 minutes. Fold in 1-1/2 cups of chocolate chips. Pour the batter into the prepared Bundt pan and bake for 55-60 minutes. Check for doneness by inserting a toothpick in the center of the cake until the toothpick comes out clean. Let the cake set in the pan for 15 minutes, then remove it to a cooling rack.

When completely cool, dust with powdered sugar and serve.

Notes:

Use good-quality cocoa powder to make this cake, as the cocoa powder's quality affects the cake's flavor. Serve this cake with sweetened whipped cream, vanilla ice cream, or gelato.

Easy Dutch Upside Down Apple Spice Cake

Makes a 9" x 13" cake

This tasty, contemporary apple-spice version of an upside-down pineapple cake is easy to make. The cake can be served as a snack or a simple party cake. Flip the cake upside down to reveal its caramelized apples, or dust the top with powdered sugar and serve it warm from the pan, accompanied with sweetened whipped cream or ice cream. This recipe wasn't found in any Crockett community cookbooks.

For the cake:
One spice cake mix
1/4 cup unsalted butter
1/2 cup brown sugar
1/2 teaspoon ground cinnamon
4 cups of apples, peeled and thinly sliced

Make the cake:
Preheat the oven to 350 degrees F. Make sure all ingredients are at room temperature.

Coat the cake pan with shortening. Cut a piece of parchment paper for the bottom of the cake pan and place it in the pan. Grease and coat the cake pan and the parchment paper with flour and set it aside.

Peel, core, and thinly slice the apples, then set them aside. Melt the butter and blend it with the brown sugar and cinnamon. Spread the mixture over the bottom of the cake pan. Arrange the apples over the sugar mixture, then set the pan aside.

Prepare the cake batter, following the directions noted on the box. Pour the batter over the apples, covering them with batter and spreading it evenly. Bake the cake for 45 to 50 minutes or until done. Check for doneness by inserting a toothpick in the center of the cake until it comes out clean.

Cool the cake in the pan for fifteen minutes, and then turn the cake upside down on a serving tray. Peel the parchment paper away and serve the cake warm.

Fantastic
Lemon Cake

Makes a large Bundt cake

Fresh lemons found in abundance on numerous trees that dot the hillsides of Crockett and Valona are critical to the success of this recipe. Refreshing on a hot summer day with fresh fruit or ice cream or comforting with a cup of tea in the winter, this lemon cake has a sweet yet tangy flavor that's not to be missed.

This specific cake wasn't found in any of the Crockett community cookbooks. Still, several similar "convenience" lemon cakes made from cake and pudding mixes are included.

For the cake:
2-3/4 cups all-purpose flour
1/2 teaspoon salt
Two teaspoons of baking powder
1 cup unsalted butter (2 cubes)
2 cups granulated sugar
Four large eggs
1 cup milk

281

Two tablespoons grated lemon peel

For the glaze:
1/3 cup fresh lemon juice
3/4 cups granulated sugar

Make the cake:
Preheat the oven to 350 degrees F. Make sure all ingredients are at room temperature.

Coat a 2-quart Bundt or tube cake pan with shortening and dust it with flour.

Combine the flour, baking powder, and salt in a medium bowl and set the mixture aside.

In the bowl of an electric mixer, cream the butter with the granulated sugar at medium speed until light and fluffy, about 5 minutes. Beat in the eggs one at a time. Reduce the speed to low and add the dry ingredients alternately with milk, beginning and ending with the flour mixture. Do not overbeat the batter. Fold in the grated lemon peel.

Pour the batter into the prepared pan and bake. When the cake has been baked for 45 minutes, check for doneness by inserting a toothpick in the center until the toothpick comes out clean.

Cool the cake in the pan for 5 minutes before removing it to a wire rack.

Make the glaze:
After removing the cake from the pan, prepare the glaze by mixing the lemon juice and sugar. Brush the glaze over the hot cake, using all the glaze. Cool the cake completely and serve.

Harvey Wallbanger Bundt Cake

Makes one Bundt cake

This contemporary, convenient, easy-to-make cake is sweet and tangy, like the cocktail. It was popular during the 1970s. It is included in the Italian Catholic Federation's *Good Things to Eat* community cookbook, published in Crockett in 1976.

The foodtimeline.org website notes that the Harvey Wallbanger cocktail originated in 1968 and the cake in 1973. The cocktail was developed at a Southern California surfing hangout - Pancho's Bar in Manhattan Beach, and is a mixture of vodka, Galliano Italian liqueur, ice, and orange juice. Other food historians have found no evidence of the bar, the cocktail's association with Southern California, or surfing. Both the cocktail and the cake, whose stories have become urban legends, may have been developed as a corporate marketing campaign to boost Galliano's sales, which are said to have increased by 40% in one year.

Whatever its history, this is a delicious cake!

For the cake:
18.25 ounces of yellow cake mix or 15.25 ounces of cake

mix with an additional 3 ounces (or six tablespoons) of the blend noted in "Recipes."
One small, 3.4-ounce package of instant vanilla pudding
Four large eggs at room temperature
1 cup vegetable oil
1/4 cup Galliano liqueur
1/4 cup Vodka
3/4 cup orange juice

For the glaze:
Two tablespoons of Galliano liqueur
Two tablespoons Vodka
Two tablespoons of orange juice
1 cup confectioners' sugar

Make the cake:
Preheat the oven to 350 degrees F. Make sure all ingredients are at room temperature.

Grease and flour a two-quart bundt pan and set it aside.

Combine the cake mix and the pudding mix in an electric mixer bowl. Blend the eggs, vegetable oil, Galliano, Vodka, and orange juice. Beat the batter for 4 minutes until it is thick and smooth.

Pour the batter into the prepared Bundt pan and bake it for one hour or until done. Check for doneness by inserting a toothpick in the center of the cake until it comes out clean. Cool the cake in the pan for 10 minutes, remove it, and place it on a cooling rack.

Prepare the glaze and spoon it over the cake while it is warm. Cool and serve.

Make the glaze:
Combine the Galliano, Vodka, and orange juice with the

confectioners' sugar and blend until smooth, ensuring no lumps. Spoon it over the warm cake.

Notes:

Serve this cake alone or with sweetened whipped cream, vanilla ice cream, or gelato.

.

Lemon Chiffon Cake

Makes an Angel Food Cake

The Lemon Chiffon Cake is an easy-to-make convenience cake bursting with lemon flavor. Serve it sprinkled with powdered sugar or as a snack or tea cake with a favorite jam, marmalade, or lemon curd. Pair it with vanilla-flavored or lemon-flavored whipped cream, gelato, berries, mascarpone cream, cream cheese, or buttercream frosting, and it's a party cake. The recipe wasn't found in any Crockett community cookbooks.

For the cake:
One package of Angel Food Cake mix (18 ounces of mix)
Four eggs
1/4 cup all-purpose flour
3/4 cup vegetable oil
Three tablespoons grated lemon rind
1 cup water
1/2 teaspoon vanilla extract

Make the cake:
Move the oven rack to the oven's lowest position and

preheat the oven to 350 degrees F. Ensure all the ingredients are at room temperature and that 18 ounces of cake mix are in the box. If there are less than 18 ounces, add another 3 ounces of mix or use the cake mix upsizer noted in Part 3, Chapter Eleven.

Add the cake mix, eggs, all-purpose flour, vegetable oil, grated lemon rind, water, and vanilla extract to the bowl of an electric mixer. Beat the ingredients at a low speed for 30 seconds, then increase the speed to medium and beat for an additional minute.

Pour the batter into an ungreased angel food cake pan and bake it for 37-47 minutes. The cake is made when the top is golden brown and feels dry, not sticky.

Remove the cake from the oven and quickly turn it upside down onto the neck of a glass bottle, such as a wine bottle, until it is completely cool. This is important. Not doing so will cause the cake to deflate.

When the cake is cool, run a sharp knife around the pan's edge and stem and remove the cake from the pan. Cut the cake with a serrated knife and store it covered.

Peach Upside-Down Cake

Makes an 8" square or round cake

This vintage variation on an upside-down pineapple cake is called a "California Peach Upside Down Cake." The cake can be served as a snack or a simple party cake. Flip the cake upside down to reveal its luscious peach and marmalade layers. Alternatively, dust the top with powdered sugar and serve it warm in the pan, accompanied by sweetened whipped cream or ice cream. This cake wasn't included in any Crockett community cookbooks.

For the cake:
1-1/2 cups fresh or canned cling peach slices
1/2 cup orange marmalade
1/3 cup unsalted butter
1/2 cup granulated sugar
One large egg
1-1/4 cups sifted cake flour
1-1/2 teaspoons baking powder
1/2 cup orange juice
1/2 teaspoon grated orange rind

Make the cake:

Preheat the oven to 350 degrees F. Make sure all ingredients are at room temperature.

Coat the cake pan with shortening. Cut a piece of parchment paper for the bottom of the cake pan. Grease and coat the cake pan and the parchment paper with flour and set it aside.

If using canned peaches, drain them thoroughly and slice them thinly. Remove the skins and pit and slice them thinly if using fresh peaches. Spread the marmalade evenly on the bottom of the pan and arrange the peaches in rows or a design.

Cream the butter and sugar together, then blend in the slightly beaten egg. Beat thoroughly. Sift the cake flour, baking powder, and salt together and add it to the beaten mixture alternately with the orange juice and the rind. Pour the batter carefully over the peaches and spread it evenly with an offset spatula.

Bake for 45-50 minutes. Check for doneness by inserting a toothpick in the center of the cake until it comes out clean. Remove the cake from the oven and cool it on a rack. When cool, carefully invert the pan onto a serving plate and remove the parchment paper.

Cut the cake into squares and serve.

Notes:

To make an extraordinary celebration party cake, bake this cake twice, arrange the layers one on top of the other, and dust the top with powdered sugar.

Quick Lemon Cake

Makes a 9" x 13" cake, or a two-quart Bundt cake

This easy-to-make refreshing lemon cake is sweet, moist, and flavorful. It wasn't included in any of the Crockett community cookbooks.

For the cake:
One small, 3.4-ounce package of lemon or raspberry Jello
18.25 ounces of yellow cake mix or 15.25 ounces of cake mix with an additional 3 ounces (or six tablespoons) of the blend noted in Chapter Twelve, "Recipes."
3/4 cup boiling water
Four large eggs
3/4 cup vegetable oil

For the glaze:
1 cup powdered sugar
4-5 tablespoons fresh lemon juice (about three lemons)

Make the cake:
Preheat the oven to 350 degrees F. Grease and flour the cake pan, and line the bottom with parchment paper if using

a 9" x 13" pan. Set the prepared pan aside.

Mix the yellow cake mix, boiling water, and vegetable oil in an electric mixer bowl. Stir briefly to combine. Add eggs one time, beating after each addition. Beat for 2 minutes.

Pour the batter into the prepared pan and bake the cake for about 35 minutes. Check for doneness by inserting a toothpick in the center of the cake until it comes out clean. When the cake is done, remove it from the oven and cool it in the pan on a cooling rack for fifteen minutes.

Make the glaze:

Make the glaze by sifting the powdered sugar to prevent lumps and combining it with lemon juice. While the cake is still warm, poke holes all over the top using a fork or a skewer. Pour 1 cup of the glaze over the cake and let it set before serving.

Sherry Wine Cake

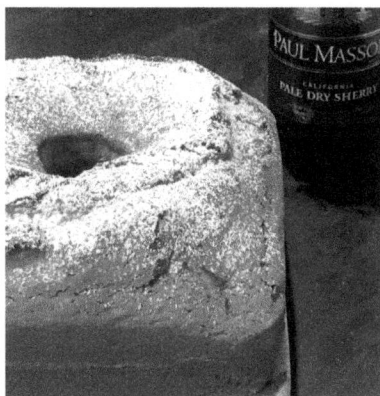

Makes a Bundt cake or cake in a tube pan

With the unusual addition of dry sherry wine and nut-meg, the flavor of this easy-to-make delicious snack cake, or understated party cake, is surprisingly complex. Finished with powdered sugar, serve it simply or with fresh fruit and sweetened, heavy whipping cream. This cake appears to be a variation of the Sherry Wine Cake, popular in Crockett and Valona during the 1960s and 1970s. Its recipe was included in two Crockett Community cookbooks.

For the cake:
18.25 ounces of yellow cake mix, or 15.25 ounces of cake mix with an additional 3 ounces (or six tablespoons) of the blend noted in "Recipes."
One small 3.4-ounce package of instant lemon pudding mix
Four large eggs at room temperature
3/4 cup vegetable oil
3/4 cup dry sherry wine
One teaspoon of ground nutmeg

Make the cake:

Preheat the oven to 350 degrees F. Grease and flour the bottom only of a tube cake pan. Do not grease and flour the sides. If using a tube pan, cut a piece of parchment paper to fit the pan's bottom to ensure the cake can be easily removed. If using a Bundt pan, grease and flour the pan. Make sure all ingredients are at room temperature.

Beat the eggs until they are thick and creamy. Add the remaining ingredients and beat for ten minutes.

Bake for 45 minutes or until done. Check for doneness by inserting a toothpick into the center of the cake until it comes out clean. Leave the cake in the pan for 15 minutes, remove it, and cool it on a wire rack. When the cake is cool, sift it with powdered sugar.

Sour Cream Pound Cake

Makes a large Bundt cake

This classic vintage recipe makes a deliciously rich, large cake. The sugar and butter combine to create a tasty crust contrasting with the moist, dense interior crumb. The recipe was found in *The Art of Cooking in Crockett, a* community cookbook published by the Carquinez Women's Club.

For the cake:
3 cups all-purpose flour, sifted
1/4 teaspoon baking soda
Pinch of salt
3/4 pound, or three cubes, of unsalted butter at room temperature
3 cups granulated sugar
Four teaspoons of baking soda
Six eggs separated
One teaspoon of almond or vanilla extract
1 cup sour cream

Make the cake:

Preheat the oven to 300 degrees F. Make sure all ingredients are at room temperature.

Coat the bottom of a 2-quart Bundt or tube cake pan with shortening and dust it with flour.

Combine the sifted flour with the baking soda and salt and set the mixture aside.

In the bowl of an electric mixer, cream the butter with 3 cups of granulated sugar until light and fluffy, about 4 minutes. Add the egg yolks and the flavoring to the butter mixture. Add flour and baking soda to the cream mixture. The batter will be very thick. Add the sour cream and mix well.

Add the egg whites with a pinch of salt to a clean electric mixer bowl and beat until stiff.

Hand-fold the beaten egg whites into the batter, then pour the batter into the prepared pan. Bake for 1-1/2 to 2 hours.

When the cake has been baked for 1-1/2 hours, check for doneness by inserting a toothpick in the center until the toothpick comes out clean. Cool the cake in the pan for 15 minutes before removing it to a wire rack to cool completely.

Notes:

Any flavoring can be used, including lemon or rum. Finish the cake with powdered sugar and unsweetened cocoa powder and serve it plain with sweetened heavy whipped cream, vanilla ice cream, gelato, or fresh summer fruit.

References and Suggested Reading

Chapter One: Crockett's Distant Past

Crockett History
Billeci, David. <u>Crockett and Its People</u>. Research by Celia Carmichael. Crockett Improvement Association, Crockett, California, 1981.

Boyer, Richard. "A Short History of Crockett". Crockett Historical Society, 1997.

Boyer, Dick. "Crockett's Beginning: The Old Homestead." *Crockett Signal*, Crockett, California, Dan Robertson, Editor, Date unknown.

Boyer, Dick. "Mother Edwards: Pioneer Woman and Crockett Founder." *Crockett Signal*, Crockett, California, Dan Robertson, Editor, June 1990.

Burt, Harriett. "Don Ignacio Martinez: Rancho Culture." *Martinez News-Gazette*, Martinez, California, June 10, 2018. Accessed on August 28, 2023. https://martinezgazette.com/don-ignacio-martinez-rancho-culture/

"California Seaports: Crockett. Seaports – Sea Captains." Accessed on May 29, 2024. https://www.maritime-heritage.org/index.html

"Crockett, California." Wikipedia. Last edited on July 16, 2020. Accessed on August 1, 2020.
https://en.wikipedia.org/w/index.php?title=Crockett_California&oldid=968016015*

"Crockett Hills Regional Park. East Bay Regional Park District." Accessed on May 29, 2024.
https://www.ebparks.org/parks/crockett hills/

"Edwards, Thomas." Contra Costa County – Tuolumnae-Inyo County CA Archives Biographies, Native Sons of the Golden West, April 8, 1812 – February 15, 1883. Accessed on May 29, 2024.
http://www.usgw archives.net/copyright.htm.
http://www.usgwarchives.net/ca/cafiles.htm

"Edwards, Thomas." History of Contra Costa County. 1926. Accessed on May 29, 2024.
http://files.usgwarchives.net/ca/contracosta/bios/edwards920bs.txt

History of Crockett, California, From The History of Contra Costa County, California. F. J. Hulaniski, Editor Berkeley, California, The Elms Publishing Co., Inc., 1917. Accessed on May 29, 2024.
http://genealogytrails.com/cal/costa/books/history_of_cc_c hapter31.html

Olsen, Keith G. "A Tree Grows in Crockett. Start-Up Days for Crockett the Town." *Crockett Signal*, Crockett, California.

Olsen, Keith G. "Rooted and Intertwined. The Crockett Banyan Tree." *Crockett Signal*, Crockett, California, March 2002.

Robinson, John V. Images of America, Crockett, San Francisco, California, Arcadia Publishing, 2004.

Staehle, Melba. "History of Crockett & Resources." Unpublished. Courtesy of the Crockett Historical Society and Museum. Undated.

Wong, Kathleen. "Carquinez Breakthrough." *Bay Nature* September 20, 2006. Accessed on October 25, 2023. https://baynature.org/article/carquinez-breakthrough/

Crockett's Indigenous People

Jones, Douglas A. "Ritual and Religion in the Ohlone Cultural Area of Central California." A thesis presented to the Department of Anthropology, San Jose State University, December 2015.

"Karkin." Wikipedia. Last modified April 27, 2020. Accessed July 2, 2020. https://en.wikipedia.org/w/index.php?title=Karkin.

"Remains of the Day. A Native American Burial Discovered in San Francisco is Shrouded in a Fog of Acrimony." *Anthropology Now*. April 26, 2016. Accessed on September 26, 2023. https://anthronow.com/2016/04/26

"San Francisco Bay Shellmounds." Phoebe A. Hearst Museum of Anthropology. Accessed on June 8, 2020. https:hearstmuseum.berkeley.edu/shellmounds

The Mexican Vaqueros
Haeber, Jonathan. "Vaqueros: The First Cowboys of the Open Range." *National Geographic*, August 15, 2003. Accessed on May 29, 2024.
https://www.nationalgeographic.com

Livingston, Phil. "The History of the Vaquero." *Cowboy*. February 13, 2017. Accessed on May 29, 2024.
https://www.americancowboy.com

"Vaquero." Wikipedia. Last modified June 2, 2020. Accessed on July 2, 2020.
https:/en.Wikipedia.org/w/index.php?title=Vaquero

Bernardo Fernandez
"The Fernandez Mansion." The Pinole History Museum. Accessed on June 8, 2020.
https://www.pinolehistorymuseum.org/news-events/the-fernandez-mansion.html

C&H Sugar Refining Company
"Alexander & Baldwin." Wikipedia. Accessed on May 29, 2024.
https://en.wikipedia.org/w/index.php?title=Alexander_%2
6_Baldwin&oldid=100957010 6"

ASR Group, C&H Sugar Holiday Greeting Card. December 2020.

REFERENCES

Billeci, David. Crockett and Its People. Research by Celia Carmichael. Crockett Improvement Association, Crockett, California, 1981.

"C&H Sugar Refining Company - American Sugar Processing and Distribution." Wikipedia. Accessed on May 28, 2024.
https://en.wikipedia.org/wiki/California_and_Hawaiian_Sugar_Company

"Claus Spreckels." Wikipedia. Accessed on January 30, 2021
https://en.wikipedia.org/w/index.php?title=Claus_Spreckels&oldid=1002864529

Emmet, Boris, Ph.D. The California and Hawaiian Sugar Refining Corporation. A Study of the Origin, Business Policies, and Management of a Co-operative Refining and Distributing Organization. Graduate School of Business, Stanford, California, Stanford University Press, 1928.

Hayes, Keri. "A Small Town's Sweet Sorrow." *East Bay Express*, Oakland, California, May 15, 2002.

Rafkin, Louise. "The C&H Sign." *The New York Times*, New York, New York, September 17, 2011

Carquinez Straits Maritime History
"A Woman Springs From the Ferry Deck. Mystery of the Steamer Garden City During a Night Trip to Alameda." The Library of Congress, Chronicling America, *The San Francisco Call*, San Francisco, December 14, 1898.

301

https://chroniclingamerica.loc.gov

"Clipper Ships." Encyclopedia.com. Accessed on October 19, 2023. https://www.encyclopedia.com/history/united-states-and-canada/us-history/clipper-ships#

"Clipper Ships. The Geography of Transport Systems." Accessed on October 19, 2023. https://transportgeography.org/contents/chapter1/emergence-of-mechanized-transportations-systems/clipper-ship/

"Coxey's Army Marches on Washington – The Gilded Age." *American Experience.* Accessed on May 29, 2024. https://ca.pbslearningmedia.org/resource/
Evanosky, Dennis. "Alameda in History: The South Pacific Coast Railroad's Lost Ferries." Issue No. 4, Fall, 2015. https://alamedamuseum.org/wp-content/uploads/2013/12/AMQ_2015_Fall.pdf

"Ferries of San Francisco Bay." Wikipedia. Accessed on May 23, 2023 https://en.wikipedia.org/wiki/Ferries_of_San_Francisco_Bay

"Gone But Not Forgotten." *Oakland Tribune.* Oakland, California, July 25, 1948. https://www.newspapers.com

Grinspan, Jon. "How a Ragtag Bank of Reformers Organized the First Protest March on Washington, D.C.." *Smithsonian,* May 1, 2014. Accessed on May 29, 2024. https://www.smithsonianmag.com/smithsonian-institution/how-ragtag-band-reformers-organized-first-protest-march-washington-dc-180951270/

"Honored Ferry Boat." *Oakland Tribune*, Oakland, California, January 28, 1940. Page 39. http://newspapers.com

"Jack London." <u>Wikipedia</u>. Accessed on May 23, 2023. https://en.wikipedia.org/wiki/Jack_London

"Log Raft Aground in Oakland Harbor." The Library of Congress, Chronicling America. *The San Francisco Call*, San Francisco, California, September 18, 1902. Accessed on May 29, 2024. https://chroniclingamerica.loc.gov

"Nebraskan Characterizes Roosevelt as Audacious, Impertinent and Impudent." The Library of Congress, Chronicling America. *The San Francisco Call*, San Francisco, California, September 26, 1912. Accessed on May 29, 2024. https://chroniclingamerica.loc.gov

Olsen, Keith G. "The Garden City is Burning." Contra Costa County Historical Society *Bulletin*. Summer 2015. Page 1.

"Paddle Wheel Ends His Life." The Library of Congress, Chronicling America. *The San Francisco Call*, San Francisco, California, February 24, 1902. Accessed on May 29, 2024. https://chroniclingamerica.loc.gov

"Reception of General Grant – The New and Elegant Steamer Garden City." *Oakland Tribune*, Oakland, California, Wednesday, September 17, 1879, page 2.

https://www.newspapers.com

"Schooner Goes Aground." The Library of Congress, Chronicling America. *The San Francisco Call*, San Francisco, California, January 10, 1908. Accessed on May 29, 2024. https://chroniclingamerica.loc.gov

Schwartz, Katrina. "How Did an 184-Foot Shipwreck Wind Up Grounded in the Carquinez Strait?" *Bay Curious*, January 27, 2022. Accessed on May 29, 2024. https://www.kqed.org/news/11902622/how-did-a-184-foot-shipwreck-wind-up-grounded-in-the-carquinez-strait

"Seeks Death in Ferry's Furnace." The Library of Congress, Chronicling America. *The San Francisco Call*, San Francisco, California, April 8, 1909. Accessed on May 29, 2024. https://chroniclingamerica.loc.gov

"The Garden City. A New Ferry Boat Launched in the Bay." *Oakland Tribune*, Oakland, California, Monday, June 23, 1879. Page 3. https://www.newspapers.com

"The Garden City Grazes a Schooner." The Library of Congress, Chronicling America. *The Morning Call*, San Francisco, California, June 12, 1893. Accessed on May 29, 2024. https://chroniclingamerica.loc.gov

"The New Ferry Steamer, Garden City, is to be Laid With Tracks…." *Oakland Tribune*, Oakland, California, November 20, 1879, page 2. https://www.newspapers.com

"The Steamer Garden City Will Leave the Foot of Broadway…," *Oakland Tribune,* Oakland, California, September 15, 1879, page 3. https://www.newspapers.com

"Wreckage of the S.S. Garden City, Crockett, California." Accessed on July 2, 2020 https://www.atlasobscura.com/places/wreck-of-the-ss-garden-city

Eckley, California
"Eckley, California." Wikipedia. Last edited on March 1, 2020. https://en.wikipedia.org

Crockett's Bridges
"Al Zampa." Wikipedia. Accessed on May 23, 2023. https://en.wikipedia.org/wiki/Al_Zampa

"Alfred Zampa Memorial Bridge Celebrates 15 Years." Last modified November 22, 2018. Accessed July 21, 2020. http://alzampabridge.com/

"Carquinez Bridge." Wikipedia. Last modified May 16, 2020. Accessed June 2, 2020. https://en.wikipedia.org/wiki/CarquinezBridge#Alfred_Zampa_Memorial Bridge. (2003 replacement span)

"This Day in History, May 21. Charles Lindbergh Completes the First Solo, Nonstop Transatlantic Flight." History.com. Last modified May 19, 2020. Accessed June 2, 2020 https://www.history.com/this-day-in-history/lindbergh-lands-in-paris

Gold Rush Entrepreneurs
"Ghirardelli Chocolate San Francisco Heritage." Domenico Ghirardelli. Accessed on May 29, 2024. https://www.ghirardelli.com/about-ghirardelli

"Gold Rush Entrepreneurs," *Economics in History*, McDougal Littell Inc. Inc., Accessed May 29, 2024. https://www.livingston.org/cms/lib4/NJ01000562/Centricity/Domain/813/Gold_Rush_Entrepreneurs.pdf

"The Story of Levi Strauss." Levi Strauss and Company. Accessed on June 8, 2020. https://www.levistrauss.com/2013/03/14/the-story-of-levi-strauss/

Chapter Two: Crockett Becomes a Company Town

George Morrison Rolph
Billeci, David. Crockett and Its People. Research by Celia Carmichael. Crockett Improvement Association, Crockett, California, 1981.

Boyer, Richard. "A Short History of Crockett". Crockett Historical Society, 1997.

"Four Brothers, Including Governor, Are Pallbearers at Simple Private Rites." *Oakland Tribune*, Oakland, California, July 23, 1932, Page 2. https://newspapers.org

"George M. Rolph Paid Tribute by Crockett Pioneer at Dedication." *Honolulu Star-Bulletin*, Honolulu, Hawaii, September 23, 1931. Page 24.

https://www.newspapers.com

"Governor Rolph's Brother Dies at Stanford Hospital." *The Modesto Bee*, Modesto, California, July 20, 1932, Page 11. Accessed on May 23, 2023. Newspapers.com

Martin, Chelse. "Save a loaf a week, help win the War": Food Conservation and World War I. Remembering WWI. Accessed on May 23, 2023. https://rememberingwwi.villanova.edu/food-conservation/

Rolph, George Morrison. Something About Sugar: Its History, Growth, Manufacture and Distribution. San Francisco, California, John J. Newbegin, Publisher, 1917.

"Rolph Park Opens October 12. Memorial Retreat to be Dedicated at Crockett." *The Honolulu Advertiser*, Honolulu, Hawaii, September 29, 1935. Page 4. https://www.newspapers.com

"Rolph Rites to be Held at S.F. Home." *Oakland Tribune*, Oakland, California, July 22, 1932, Page 13. https://newspapers.org

James Rolph
"California Governor James Rolph." National Governors Association. Accessed on May 29, 2024. https://www.nga.org/governor/james-rolph/

Chan, Loren B. "California During the Early 1930s: The Administration of Governor James Rolph, Jr., 1931-1934." Southern California Quarterly (1981) 63 (3): 262–282,

October 1, 1981.
https://doi.org/10.2307/41170950

Issel, William, and Cherny, Robert. "The Reign of Rolph, 1911-1932." *San Francisco 1865-1932*, Chapter 8, "Politics During the Reign of Rolph," 1911-1932. Accessed on May 29, 2024. https://foundsf.org/index

"James Rolph." Wikipedia. Accessed on May 29, 2024. https://en.wikipedia.org/wiki/James_Rolph

"Twenty-first Amendment." Encyclopaedia Britannica, Encyclopaedia Britannica, Inc. Accessed on April 18, 2020. https://www.britannica.com/topic/Twenty-first-Amendment.

C&H Sugar Refining Company
Billeci, David. Crockett and Its People. Research by Celia Carmichael. Crockett Improvement Association, Crockett, California, 1981.

Boyer, Richard. "A Short History of Crockett". Crockett Historical Society, 1997.

"C&H Sugar Refinery." Wikipedia. Accessed on May 29, 2024.
http://en.wikipedia.org/wiki/California_and_Hawaiian_Sugar_Company

Emmet, Boris, Ph.D. The California and Hawaiian Sugar Refining Corporation. A Study of the Origin, Business Policies, and Management of a Co-operative Refining and

Distributing Organization. Graduate School of Business, Stanford, California, Stanford University Press, 1928.

Hotel Crockett
Billeci, David. Crockett and Its People. Research by Celia Carmichael. Crockett Improvement Association, Crockett, California, 1981.

Boyer, Richard. "A Short History of Crockett". Crockett Historical Society, 1997.

Tenney Terrace
Boyer, Richard. "A Short History of Crockett". Crockett Historical Society, 1997.

Tenney, Edward Davies, January 26, 1859. Statewide County Hawaii Archives Biographies. Accessed on May 29, 2024. http://files.usgwarchives.net/hi/statewide/bios/tenney583bs.txt

C&H Company House
"C&H Will Build Fine Residence. Will be Home of General Manager Rolph. *Crockett Signal*, Crockett, California, March 23, 1917. Archives of Dr. and Mrs. Mervyn Silverman.

Thomas, Diane Bottini. "C&H Company House and Guest Cottage History." April 1992.

Crockett Club
Billeci, David. Crockett and Its People. Research by Celia

Carmichael. Crockett Improvement Association, Crockett, California, 1981.

Boyer, Richard. "A Short History of Crockett". Crockett Historical Society, 1997.

Crockett Community Auditorium
"Community Auditorium Will be Opened on February 25." *Crockett Signal*, Crockett, California, February 13, 1920.

"New Community Auditorium to be Dedicated Wednesday." *Crockett Signal*, Crockett, California, February 20, 1920.

"New Community Auditorium Dedicated." *Crockett Signal*, Crockett, California, February 27, 1920.

Wilson, Ron. "Crockett Centennial Celebration." Speech researched, written, and delivered in February 2020.

The Bohemian Club
"Bohemian Grove." Wikipedia. Edited on November 26, 2020. Accessed on May 29, 2024.
https://en.wikipedia.org/w/index.php?Bohemian_Club&oldid=990868579

Flock, Elizabeth. "Bohemian Grove: Where the rich and powerful go to misbehave." *The Washington Post*, Washington, D.C., June 15, 2011. Accessed on May 29, 2024.
https://www.washingtonpost.com/blogs/blogpost/post/bohemian-grove-where-the-rich-and-powerful-go-to-misbehave/2011/06/15/AGPV1sVH_blog.html

"The Bohemian Club." Encyclopaedia Britannica, May 14, 2020. Access on February 13, 2021. https://www.britannica.com/topic/The-Bohemain-Club

The Cubelet Press
C&H News, Thursday, July 23, 1936. Crockett Historical Society

Home Building Program
Emmet, Boris, Ph.D. The California and Hawaiian Sugar Refining Corporation. A Study of the Origin, Business Policies, and Management of a Co-operative Refining and Distributing Organization. Graduate School of Business, Stanford, California, Stanford University Press, 1928.

Public Planting Program
Emmet, Boris, Ph.D. The California and Hawaiian Sugar Refining Corporation. A Study of the Origin, Business Policies, and Management of a Co-operative Refining and Distributing Organization. Graduate School of Business, Stanford, California, Stanford University Press, 1928.

Crockett Improvement Association
Billeci, David. Crockett and Its People. Research by Celia Carmichael. Crockett Improvement Association, Crockett, California, 1981.

Crockett Chamber of Commerce
https://www.crockettcalifornia.com/

Chapter Three: Italian Immigrants Arrive

C&H Sugar Refining Company
Emmet, Boris, Ph.D. The California and Hawaiian Sugar Refining Corporation. A Study of the Origin, Business Policies, and Management of a Co-operative Refining and Distributing Organization. Graduate School of Business, Stanford, California, Stanford University Press, 1928.

Krache, Maria. "Nonno in Crockett: A Man and a Company Town." *Mother Jones*. July 1976, page 11.

John Muir and Family
"Helen Muir." Sierra Club.org. Accessed on September 23, 2020. https://vault.sierraclub.org/john_muir_exhibit/people/helen_muir_bio.aspx

"Louise Strentzel Muir." Sierra Club.org. Accessed on September 23, 2020. https://vault.sierraclub.org/john_muir_exhibit/people/louie_muir_bio.aspx
Muir, John, Deed, John Muir, et al. to Carlo Magnaghi, dated November 16, 1912.

John Strentzel
"John Strentzel." Sierra Club.org. Accessed on September 23, 2020.
https://vault.sierraclub.org/john_muir_exhibit/people/john_strentzel.aspx

Crockett History
Robinson, John V. Images of America, Crockett, San Francisco, California, Arcadia Publishing, 2004.

Valona History
"Valona." Google Earth. Accessed on September 12, 2020.
http://googleearth.com/Valona

Italian Immigration/Immigrants
Cannato, Vincent J. "What Sets Italian Americans Off From Other Immigrants?" *Humanities,* National Endowment for the Humanities, January/February 2015, Volume 36, Number 1.

Chicago Union Station. Accessed on April 26, 2021
https://en.m.wikipedia.org/wiki/Chicago_Union_Station

Molnar, Alexandra. "From Europe to America: Immigration Through Family Tales." History of Italian Immigration. December 15, 2010. Accessed on August 3, 2020.
http://mthdyoke.edu

Carlo Magnaghi Family
Ancestry.com

Alessandro Pagni Family
Ancestry.com

Ben Zuppan
Billeci, David. Crockett and Its People. Research by Celia Carmichael. Crockett Improvement Association, Crockett, California, 1981.

Chapter Four: Creating an Italian Village in Valona

C&H Sugar Refining Company

Emmet, Boris, Ph.D. The California and Hawaiian Sugar Refining Corporation. A Study of the Origin, Business Policies, and Management of a Co-operative Refining and Distributing Organization. Graduate School of Business, Stanford, California, Stanford University Press, 1928.

Krache, Maria. "Nonno in Crockett: A Man and a Company Town." *Mother Jones*. July 1976, page 11.

Italian Immigration/Immigrants

Cannato, Vincent J. "What Sets Italian Americans Off From Other Immigrants?" *Humanities*, National Endowment for the Humanities, January/February 2015, Volume 36, Number 1.

Mangione, Jerre and Morreale, Ben. *La Storia. Five Centuries of the Italian American Experience.* Harper Perennial, New York. 1992.

Molnar, Alexandra. "From Europe to America: Immigration Through Family Tales." History of Italian Immigration. December 15, 2010. Accessed on August 3, 2020. http://mthdyoke.edu

Roberto, Laura E. and Sciorra, Joseph. New Italian Migrations to the United States. Volume 1: Politics and History Since 1945. University of Illinois Press. 2017.

Roberto, Laura E. and Sciorra, Joseph. New Italian Migra-tions to the United States. Volume 12: Art and Culture Since 1945. University of Illinois Press. 2017.

World War II
"Blitzkrieg (Lightning War)." United States Holocaust Me-morial Museum, Holocaust Encyclopedia. Accessed on May 31, 2023.
https://encyclopedia.ushmm.org/content/en/article/blitzkri eg-lightning-war

"Blitzkrieg." History.com Editors. Updated: December 12, 2022. Original: October 14, 2009. Accessed on May 31, 2023. https://www.history.com/topics/world-war-ii/blitzkrieg

Italian Internment
DiStasi, Lawrence. Branded. How Italian Immigrants Be-came 'Enemies' During World War II. Sanniti Publications, Bolinas, CA. 2016

DiStasi, Lawrence, Editor, Una Storia Segreta, "The Secret History of Italian American Evacuation and Internment During World War II." Heydey, Berkeley, California, 2001.

Fox, Stephen. The Unknown Internment. "An Oral History of the Relocation of Italian Americans During World War II." T. Wayne Publishers, a Division of G.K. Hall & Co., Boston, MA. 1990

Mangione, Jerre and Ben Morreale. La Storia. "Five Cen-turies of the Italian American Experience." Harper

Perennial, New York, New York, 1992.

Puloka, Deanne S. "The Alien Registration Act of 1940." Accessed on May 10, 2021. https://www.mckendree.edu/academics/scholars/issue13/puloka.htm.

Italian Culture/Traditions
De Bonneville, Francoise. The Book of Fine Linen. Flammarion, Paris, France. 1994.
"A Fabric Collector's Diary. Italian Linen." Accessed on May 5, 2015. http://belovedlinens.net/fabrics/Italian_linen.html.

Flower, Raymond, and Falassi, Alessandro. Culture Shock! A Guide to Customs and Etiquette in Italy. Graphic Arts Center Publishing Company. 1995

Holme, Charles, edited by. *Peasant Art in Italy*. The Studio Ltd. New York. MCMXIII.

Garrubbo, Edwin. Garrubo Guide, The Importance of Eating Italian. Garrubbo Communication, LLC. 2020. www.Garrubbo.com

Luard, Elisabeth. Sacred Food, Cooking for Spiritual Nourishment. Chicago Review Press, Chicago, Illinois, 2001

Pascali, Lara. "Two Stoves, Two Refrigerators, Due Cucine: The Italian immigrant home with two kitchens." Winterthur Museum, Garden and Library. Delaware, USA. 2006

Crockett Bass Club
"Bass Club." *Crockett Signal*, Crockett, California, May 8, 1936.

Chapter Five: Crockett's Golden Age

Lodena Edgecumbe
"About Lodena Edgecumbe," DBPedia.
https://dbpedia.org/page/Lodena_Edgecumbe

"Lodena Edgcumbe." Historical Articles of Solano County Online Database, James Kern. May 11, 2006. Accessed on May 23, 2023.
http://www.solanoarticles.com/history/index.php/weblog5 /more/lodena_edgcumbe/

"Lodena Edgecumbe." Wikipedia. Last modified on October 15, 2019. Accessed on July 3, 2020,
https://en.wikipedia.org/w/index./php?title=Lodena_Edge-cumbe

"Vallejo Kin to Fete Dancer." *Oakland Tribune*, Oakland, California, Sunday, December 19, 1926, page 70.
http://www.newspapers.com

C&H Christmas Play
"Christmas Party." *Cubelet Press*, Vol. 17, January 10, 1952. No. 1

"Season's Greetings." *Cubelet Press*, Vol. 15, January 12, 1950, No. 1

Recreation Programs for Children

"Pets & Kids." *Cubelet Press*, Vol. 17, September 25, 1952. No. 18

"Room for Play." *Cubelet Press*, Vol. 17, June 12, 1952, No. 11

Chapter Six: Unexpected Forces Drive Change

Crockett's History
Billeci, David. Crockett and Its People. Research by Celia Carmichael. Crockett Improvement Association, Crockett, California, 1981.

Boyer, Richard. "A Short History of Crockett". Crockett Historical Society, 1997.

"Crockett, California." Wikipedia. Last edited on July 16, 2020. Accessed on August 1, 2020
https://en.wikipedia.org/w/index.php?title=Crockett_California&oldid=968016015*

Robinson, John V. Images of America, Crockett, San Francisco, California, Arcadia Publishing, 2004.

C&H Sugar Refining Company
Billeci, David. Crockett and Its People. Research by Celia Carmichael. Crockett Improvement Association, Crockett, California, 1981.

Emmet, Boris, Ph.D. The California and Hawaiian Sugar Refining Corporation. A Study of the Origin, Business

Policies, and Management of a Co-operative Refining and Distributing Organization. Graduate School of Business, Stanford, California, Stanford University Press, 1928.

Rafkin, Louise. "The C&H Sign." *The New York Times*, New York, New York, September 17, 2011

Crockett's Bridges
"Al Zampa." Wikipedia. Accessed on May 23, 2023.
https://en.wikipedia.org/wiki/Al_Zampa

"Alfred Zampa Memorial Bridge Celebrates 15 Years."
Last modified November 22, 2018. Accessed July 21, 2020.
http://alzampabridge.com/

"Carquinez Bridge." Wikipedia. Last modified May 16, 2020. Accessed June 2, 2020.
https://en.wikipedia.org/wiki/CarquinezBridge#Alfred_Zampa_Memorial Bridge.

"This Day in History, May 21. Charles Lindbergh Completes the First Solo, Nonstop Transatlantic Flight." History.com. Last modified May 19, 2020. Accessed June 2, 2020
https://www.history.com/this-day-in-history/lindbergh-lands-in-paris

Crockett's Telephone System
Billeci, David. Crockett and Its People. Research by Celia Carmichael. Crockett Improvement Association, Crockett, California, 1981.
"Crockett Says Goodbye to an Old Friend." *The Cubelet*

Press, Vol. XXXV, No. 10, October 1969

"Special Telephone Directory for Crockett," Pacific Telephone. November 15, 1969.

Chapter Seven: Breaking the Sugar Ceiling

It's a Man's Man's Man's Man's World
Brown, James. "Billboard Year-End Hot 100 Chart for 1966."
https://www.musicoutfitters.com/topsongs/1966.htm
Lyrics:
https:://www.google.com/search?q=james+brown+its+a+m
ans

Chapter Eight: Packing War Sugar for Vietnam

C&H Sugar in the South Pacific during World War II
"Mail From the Boys." *Cubelet Press*. July, 1943

Vietnam War
"Cubans Give Sugar to Hanoi." *Cubelet Press*. Volume XXXI, No. 1, January 1966, page 12.

"Doing Business With the Government." *Cubelet Press*. Volume XXXII, No. 3, March, 1967, page 3.

"Marketing, the Year in Review." *Cubelet Press*. Volume XXXIV, No. 4, April, 1968.

"Request From Vietnam." *Cubelet Press*. November 1966.

C&H Family Loyalty
Cubelet Press, Volume 14, No. 4, February 24, 1949.

Perfect Attendance at the Refinery
"Perfect Attendance." *Cubelet Press*. Volume XLIII, No. 3, March 1978.

Chapter Nine: Going the Distance
"Sugar Packet," Wikipedia. Accessed on January 8, 20244. https://en.wikipedia.org/w/index.php?title"Sugar_packet &oldid=1177076112

Chapter Eleven: Researching and Testing the Recipe Collection

Women's Rights
Bailey, Dr. Jegan. "Between Two Worlds: Black Women and the Fight for Voting Rights." Suffrage in America: The 15th and 19th Amendments, National Parks Service. Accessed on May 31, 2024. https://www.nps.gov/articles/black-women-and-the-fight-for-voting-rights.htm

"'It's a Struggle They Will Wage Alone.' How Black Women Won the Right to Vote." *Time Magazine*. Accessed on February 28, 2022.

Milligan, Susan, "Stepping Through History: A Timeline of Women's Rights from 1769 to the 2017 Women's March on Washington. *US News & World Report*. January 20, 2017.

Community Cookbooks

Martyris, Nina. "How Suffragists Used Cookbooks As A Recipe For Subversion." NPR. November 5, 2015.

Moniz, Amanda. "First Community Cookbook Written for Fun, Started a Trend. American Food Roots," June 1, 2014. Accessed on January 11, 2020.
http://www.americanfoodroots.com/features/readings/first-community-cookbook-written-fun-started-trend/

"Research Tool for Culinary Historians." Cookbooks, Community. Encyclopedia.com.
Accessed on December 22, 2021. https://www.encyclopedia.com/food/encyclopedias-almanacs-transcripts-and-maps/cookbooks-community.

Stoller-Conrad, Jessica. "Long Before Social Networking, Community Cookbooks Rules The Stove." NPR. July 20, 2012. Accessed on December 22, 2021.
https://www.npr.org/sections/thesalt/2012/07/18

Tillie, Lola. "The Billfold Goes to the Archives: Community Cookbooks. November 9, 2018.

Cake History

Oliver, Lynne. "The Food Timeline." https://www.foodtimeline.org

Recipe or Receipt

"Receipt vs Recipe." *Grammarist*. Accessed on January 31, 2022.
https://grammarist.com/usage/receipt-vs-recipe/

"When a Recipe was a 'Receipt.'" <u>Merriam-Webster Dictionary</u>. Accessed on January 31, 2022. https://merriam-webster.com/words-at-play/recipe-vs-receipt-usage-word-history

Civil Rights in the United States
Block, Melissa. "Yes, Women Could Vote After The 19th Amendment – But Not All Women. Or Men." NPR Morning Edition. August 26, 2020.

"Lead-up to the Civil Rights Act." Civil Rights Act of 1964. History.com. Accessed on February 28, 2022. https://www.history.com/topics/black-history/civil-rights-act

Cake Mix "Up-Sizer"
Adapted from the Better Homes & Gardens New Cook Book for White and Yellow Cake Recipes. Food.com. Accessed on July 9, 2023. https://www.food.com/recipe/cake-mix-quot-up-sizer-quot-531108

List of Images

- Crockett Lumber Company, Crockett Historical Society Collection

Chapter Two: Crockett Becomes a Company Town

- George Morrison Rolph, Crockett Historical Society Collection
- Hotel Crockett, Crockett Historical Society Collection
- Tenney Terrace, Crockett Historical Society Collection
- C&H Sugar Company House, Crockett Historical Society Collection
- The Crockett Club, Crockett Historical Society Collection
- The Crockett Club Interior, Crockett Historical Society Collection
- Crockett Swim Pass, Pagni Family Artifacts
- Crockett Club Swimming Pool #1, Crockett Historical Society Collection
- Crockett Club Swimming Pool #2, Crockett Historical Society Collection
- Crockett Community Auditorium, Crockett Historical Society Collection
- Alexander Park: PH.14110, Sharkey Family Collection 2011.36, CCCHS Special Collections
- Message from C&H Sugar President Sullivan, *Cubelet Press*, Vol. 1. No. 1, Thursday, July 23, 1936, Crockett Historical Society Collection

Chapter Three: Italian Immigrants Arrive

- Virginia Fassi, Magnaghi Family Photo Collection
- Magnaghi/Muir Property Deed, Magnaghi Family Artifacts

- Magnaghi Family Home on Fifth Avenue, Crockett, CA, Magnaghi Family Photo Collection
- C&H Sugar Operating Calendar, Pagni/Magnaghi Family Artifacts
- Dr. John Theophil Strentzel: PH.2202, Louis Stein Collection, CCCHS Special Collections
- John Muir and Family: PH.2844, Louis Stein Collection, CCCHS Special Collections
- Alessandro Pagni, Pagni Family Photo Collection
- Fausto and Luisa Guidi, Pagni Family Photo Collection
- Pagni Family Passport, Pagni Family Artifacts
- Zuppan Store, Crockett Historical Society Collection
- Pagni Family Ship Ticket, Pagni Family Artifacts

Chapter Four: Creating an Italian Village in Valona
- Citizenship Book, Magnaghi Family Artifacts
- National Registration of Aliens, Magnaghi Family Artifacts
- Citizenship Program #1, Magnaghi Family Artifacts
- Citizenship Program #2, Magnaghi Family Artifacts
- Italian Cutwork Embroidery, Barbara Pagni Denton photo
- Giuseppina Pagni, Faustino Pagni Photo Collection
- Isolated Crockett, Crockett Historical Society Collection
- Mary Pini Pagni and Alessandro Pagni in the Garden, Faustino Pagni Photo Collection
- Heirloom Tomato Seeds, Barbara Pagni Denton photo
- Wine Permit, Magnaghi Family Artifacts
- Alessandro Pagni Wearing his Sleeve Garters, Faustino Pagni Photo Collection
- *Stanzing*, Ralph Pagni Photo Collection
- Dowrelio's Marina, Faustino Pagni Photo Collection

- Pagni Brothers and Their Rowboat, Faustino Pagni Photo Collection
- A. Biondi Sausage Factory Bag, Magnaghi Family Artifacts
- Nuns at St. Rose of Lima, Mary and Medoro Pagni Photo Collection

Chapter Five: Crockett's Golden Age
- Pete's Ranch, Crockett Historical Society Collection
- Cattle Branding at Pete's Ranch, Faustino Pagni Photo Collection
- Annual Garden Show, Crockett Historical Society Collection
- Room for Play, *Cubelet Press*, Vol. 17, No. 11, June 12, 1952, Crockett Historical Society Collection
- Annual Pet Show, *Cubelet Press*, Vol. 17, No. 18, September 25, 1952, Crockett Historical Society Collection
- C&H Sugar Carpenter Shop Christmas Elves, Faustino Pagni Photo Collection; photo likely taken by Mr. Swain
- Toy Giveaway, *Cubelet Press*, Vol. 15, No. 1, January 12, 1950, Crockett Historical Society Collection
- Christmas Play Audience, *Cubelet Press*, Vol. 15, No. 1, January 12, 1950, Crockett Historical Society Collection
- *Nutcracker Suite* Dolls, Faustino Pagni Photo Collection, photo likely taken by Mr. Swain
- Aldo Ray, Crockett Historical Society Collection

Chapter Six: Unexpected Forces Drive Change
- Destruction of Valona #1, Faustino Pagni Photo Collection
- Destruction of Valona #2, Faustino Pagni Photo Collection
- Destruction of Valona #3, Faustino Pagni Photo Collection

Chapter Eight: Packing War Sugar for Vietnam
- Faustino Pagni in New Guinea, World War II, *Cubelet Press*, Crockett Historical Society Collection
- Louise Magnaghi Packing Sugar, Cubelet Press, Crockett Historical Society Collection

Chapter Nine: Going the Distance
- Teabags at the Museum, Barbara Pagni Denton Photo, Crockett Historical Society Collection
- Beverly Hills Hotel Teabag, Barbara Pagni Denton Photo, Crockett Historical Society Collection
- Cube Station, *Cubelet Press*, Crockett Historical Society Collection
- Teabags Station, *Cubelet Press*, Cubelet Press, Vol. XXXI, Nos. 7-8, July-August 1966, Crockett Historical Society Collection
- Powder Mill, *Cubelet Press*, Crockett Historical Society Collection
- Louise Magnaghi Working at the Teabags Station, *Cubelet Press*, *Crockett Press*, Vol. XL, No. 8, Crockett Historical Society Collection

Chapter Ten: Researching and Testing the Recipe Collection
- Louise Magnaghi's "Mixmaster" Manual, Barbara Pagni Denton Photo

About the Author

Growing up in a family of storytellers eager to share their tales of the Old Country and their emigration and assimilation experiences, Barbara grasped early on the importance of a well-crafted, well-told story to inform, teach, and entertain. Continuing this ancient tradition, she shares her intimate knowledge of growing up in Crockett, California, a unique San Francisco Bay Area factory town. Barbara also shares stories of working women at the C&H Sugar refinery, whose stories have yet to be written. She writes about her experiences living in this small company town in the mid-twentieth century and working in this Bay Area industrial icon in the late 1960s. Barbara lived most of her life in Crockett and worked at the factory for two summers as a temporary summer hire while attending the University of California at Berkeley.

Pagni Denton lives in Crockett, California, with her husband, Ed, in a century-old cottage that offers a picturesque view of the Carquinez Straits, steep cattle pasture lands, and the rural, winding, narrow two-lane road to Port Costa. She is a retired healthcare environmental designer passionate about baking, making chocolates, writing, and gardening. In her free time, she enjoys her morning walks through the hilly Crockett neighborhoods and chatting with her neighbors in her colorful flower-filled front garden.

ABOOKS

ALIVE Book Publishing and ALIVE Publishing Group
are imprints of Advanced Publishing LLC,
3200 A Danville Blvd., Suite 204, Alamo, California 94507

Telephone: 925.837.7303
alivebookpublishing.com

Milton Keynes UK
Ingram Content Group UK Ltd.
UKHW032327221024
449917UK00004B/323